# PRE-GAṄGEŚA CONCEPT OF LIṄGAPARĀMARŚA

# PRE-GAṄGEŚA CONCEPT OF LIṄGAPARĀMARŚA

(with special reference to Śaśadhara)

*By*

BHAGABAN PANDA

BHARATIYA KALA PRAKASHAN
DELHI (INDIA)

First Edition : 2009



*Published by* **C.P. Gautam**
BHARATIYA KALA PRAKASHAN
3421-A, IInd Floor Narang Colony, Tri Nagar,
Delhi-110035. Ph. : 32967505, Telefax : 011-27393083
E-mail : bkp3421@yahoo.co.in

**ISBN : 978-81-8090-158-4**

*Printed By :*
BDH Printer at Salasar Imaging Systems,
Delhi

यं शैवास्समुपासते शिव इति ब्रह्मेति वेदान्तिनः
बौद्धाः बुद्ध इति प्रमाणपटवः कर्तेति नैयायिकाः।
अर्हन्नित्यथ जैनशासनरताः कर्मेति मीमांसकाः
सोऽयं न विदधातु वाञ्छितफलं त्रैलोक्यनाथो हरिः॥

(May Hari, the lord of three world, whom Śaivas call as *Śiva,* Vedāntins call as *Brahma,* the followers of Gautama Budha call as *Buddha,* Naiyāyikas, who are experts in the science of *pramāṇas,* call as *kartā,* (Agent of the Universe), Jainas call as *Arhat* and Mīmāṃsakas call as *Karma,* fulfill our desires).

कुतो वा नूतनं वस्तु वयमुत्प्रेक्षितुं क्षमाः।
वचोविन्यासवैचित्र्यमात्रमत्र विचार्यताम्।

—न्यायमञ्जरी—८

(We claim no originality of thinking to discover new truth but have fascinating style to express the old ones in an attractive form. Let the critics examine it for themselves.)

# CONTENTS

# PREFACE

This is the Revised Version of my Ph.D. thesis "Pre-Gaṅgeśa concept of Liṅgaparāmarśa" (With special reference to Śaśadhara) approved by the University of Pune for the award of Ph.D. degree in Sanskrit in 2002.

There are number of controversies in accepting parāmarśa as a key-factor in Inference. On the one side stands the extreme realist among which the Naiyāyika in chief, who holds clearly an objective view of the parāmarśa being an 'immediate cause of the process of Inference', which is supposed to be an important factor of our day to day life. On the other side, we have systems like Mīmāṃsā, Buddhists etc. who hold a subjective view of the concept. To them, this is just a conceptual fiction designed by the Naiyāyikas having no practical reality. It is Śaśadhara, the author of Nyāyasiddhāntadīpa, who stands in the middle keeping the realists on the one side and the idealists on the other, maintaining a relative view of the concept i.e. parāmarśa. Here, he presents the grounds of both the parties, analyses it and finally solves it. Śaśadhara, the author of Nyāyasiddhāntadīpa, a monumental treatise of the system, devoted a full chapter entitled "Liṅgaparāmarśavāda" of Nyāyasiddhāntadīpa. We have made of Pandit B.K. Motilal's addition of Nyāyasiddhāntadīpa.

It is my pleasure to record now the help I have received from various scholars in preparing this work. I sincerely hold this opportunity to express my great indebtedness to Prof. V.N. Jha, Director, Centre of Advanced Study in Sanskrit, University of Pune, my research guide, whose planned guidance canalized my efforts in a proper direction. It is Prof. Jha, who taught me the fundamentals of Navya-Nyāya language and methodology, which helped me a lot to design the present study.

I am obliged to all the members of the teaching and non-teaching staff of the department for the help I have received during my study period. I thank my seniors Dr. Yoshodhara Kar, Dr. Nilkantha Dash, Dr. Niranjan Jena. I am thankful to my friends Mr. D. Mohanty, A. Dash, J. Mishra, N. Kar and Miss. R. Nanda.

I convey my immense debt of gratitude to my brother Mr. Ramchandra Panda who ones dreamt me to be at this stage. My nieces Mamina, Ratan, my wife Manju, my daughter Sravani and my mother are the sources of my constant inspiration. It is their love and affection, which created a homely atmosphere for me to survive during my difficult days.

Finally, I thank Mr. C.P. Gautam, Publisher, Bharatiya Kala Prakashan, New Delhi, for accepting this work for publication.

Date: 15th August 2006
Amravati

**Bhagaban Panda**
Govt. Vidarbha Institute of Science
& Humanities, Amravati.
(Maharashtra)

# KEY TO TRANSLITERATION AND PRONUNCIATION

| | | Sounds like |
|---|---|---|
| अ | a | o i s*o*n |
| आ | ā | a in m*a*ster |
| इ | i | i in *i*f |
| ई | ī | ee in f*ee*d |
| उ | u | u in f*u*ll |
| ऊ | ū | oo in b*oo*t |
| ऋ | ṛ | somewhat between r and ri |
| ए | e | a in ev*a*de |
| ऐ | ai | y in my |
| ओ | o | o in *o*ver |
| औ | au | ow in n*o*w |
| क | k | k |
| ख | kh | ckh in blo*ckh*ead |
| ग | g | g (hard) |
| घ | gh | gh in lo*g-h*ut |
| ङ | ṅ | ng |
| च | c | ch (not k) |
| छ | ch | chh in cat*ch h*im |
| ज | j | j |

| | | |
|---|---|---|
| झ | jh | dgeh in he*dgeh*og |
| ञ | ñ | n (somewhat) |
| ट | ṭ | t |
| ठ | ṭh | th in an*t-h*ill |
| ड | ḍ | d |
| ढ | ḍh | dh in go*dh*ood |
| ण | ṇ | n in *un*der |
| त | t | French t |
| थ | th | th in *th*umb |
| द | d | th in *th*en |
| ध | dh | theh in brea*the h*ere |
| न | n | n |
| प | p | p |
| फ | ph | ph in loo*p-h*ole |
| ब | b | b |
| भ | bh | bh in a*bh*or |
| म | m | m |
| य | y | y |
| र | r | r |
| ल | l | l |
| व | v | v in a*v*ert |
| श | ś | sh |
| ष | ṣ | sh in *sh*ow |
| स | s | s |
| ह | h | h |
| ं | ṁ | m in hu*m* |
| : | ḥ | half h in hu*h*! |

# ABBREVIATIONS

| | |
|---|---|
| *AC* | *Anumānacintāmaṇi* |
| *AP* | *Anumāna Pramāṇa* |
| *BDB* | *Bhāratīyadarśana Bṛhatkośa* |
| BL | Buddhist Logic |
| *BP* | *Bhāṣāpariccheda* |
| *BSSB* | *Brahmasūtraśānkarabhāṣya* |
| *Di.A* | *Didhitī, Anumānakhaṇḍa* |
| *EBPM* | *Epistemology of the Bhāṭṭa school of pūrva Mīmāṁsā* |
| *EIP* | *Encyclopedia of Indian Philosophies* |
| *HIE* | *History of Indian Epistemology* |
| HIL | History of Indian Logic |
| *ICNN* | *Invariable concomitance in Navya-Nyāya* |
| *IL* | *Indian Logic* |
| *ITK* | *Indian theory of Knowledge* |
| *MM* | *Mānameyodaya* |
| *MS* | *Mīmāṁsāsūtra* |
| *NB* | *Nyāyabindu* |
| *NBh* | *Nyāyabhāṣya (Vātsāyana)* |
| *NBn* | *Nyāyabodhinī, anumānakhaṇḍa* |
| *NM* | *Nyāyamañjarī* |
| NP | *Nyāpraveśa* |
| *NPs* | *Nyāyaprakāśa* |

| | |
|---|---|
| *NR* | *Nyāyaratnākara* |
| *NS* | *Nyāyasūtra* |
| *NSG* | *Nyāyasūtra of Gotama* |
| *NSM* | *Nyāyasiddhāntamuktāvalī* |
| *NSV* | *Nyāyasūtravṛtti* |
| *NTK* | *Nyāya theory of knowledge* |
| *NV* | *Nyāyavārttika* |
| *NVTT* | *Nyāyavārttikatātparyaṭikā* |
| *NVTTP* | *Nyāyavārttikatātparyaṭikāpariśuddhi* |
| PBh | *Prasastapādabhāṣya* |
| *PP* | *Prakaraṇa panjñikā* |
| *PV* | *Pramtinavtirttika* |
| *SBD* | *Syādvādamañjarī* |
| *SBH* | *Śābarabhāṣya* |
| *SK* | *Sāṃkhyakārikā* |
| *SS* | *Sāṃkhya-sūtra* |
| *STK* | *Sāṃkhyatattvakaumudī* |
| *SV-2* | *Ślaokavārttika* |
| *TBA* | *Tarkabhaṣa, anumanakhaṇḍa* |
| *TCsnp* | *Tattvacintāmaṇi, sāmānyanirukti-prakaraṇa* |
| *TD* | *Tarkadīpikā* |
| *TM* | *Tarkāmṛta* |
| TSA | *Tarkasaṃgraha, Ammānakhaṇḍa* |

# INTRODUCTION

## GENERAL BACKGROUND

### The problem

Even a layman, after perceiving a whiff of smoke, comes to know fire. The process through which he comes to this conclusion is called *anumāna*. *Parāmarśa* is an element of that process of inference. But the *Naiyāyikas* assign a vital role to it. They hold *parāmarśa* as an 'intermediate cause of the precess of inference',[1] which is supposed to be an important factor of our day to day life, as everything does not exist within the range of our senses to feel. The definition of *parāmarśa,* given by *Naiyāyikas,* is the knowledge of probans qualified by invariable concomitance (with the probandum)[2].

On the other hand, we have systems like *Mīmāṁsā, Buddhism* etc., which have developed a keen interested in *Nyāya* system. When *Nyāya* declared that *parāmarśa* is an intermediate operation of the process of inference those systems opposed. "This is not fair to entertain a component called *parāmarśa*", argues opponents, "when the process can be explained in the following way." First of all, explains *Mimāṃsa* system, there will arise the remembrance or experience of invariable concomitance and thereafter will arise the cognition of smoke, which is located in the subject, in which there is a property called 'smokeness', which is delimitor of the state of being pervaded (by the probamdum) appears as the qualifier. Immediately after that the inferential cognition arises without any hindrance. When this can be explained in the above manner, it is cumbrousome to postulate a qualified cognition (i.e. *Parāmarśa)* in the middle[3].

To them this is just a conceptual fiction designed by *Naiyāyikas* having no practical reality[4].

When such was the standpoint of the opponents *Nyāyasiddhāntadīpa* (here after NSD) was made to settle down the whole thing. In this text, *Śaśadhara* takes up all objections, raised against *parāmarśa,* analyzes it and finally solves it.

The present work attempts to highlight the discussions made by *Śaśadhara.* To do so, I selected the seventeenth chapter of NSD i.e. *liṅgaparāmarśavāda,* translated it into English. The only reason behind this attempt is to bring those discus-sions, made by *Śaśadhara* and other logicians, into light.

An analytical look at the works on Indian logic highlights the fact that the importance of the concept of accepting *parāmarśa,* involved in the process of inference, was fully realized by a good deal of ancient as well as modern scholars. Among the ancient works the following texts can be taken into consideration.

**Survey of the works done**

1. परामर्शविचार: of महामहोपाध्याय हरिरामतर्कालंकार
2. लिङ्गपरामर्शवाद[5]
3. लिङ्गपरामर्शवाद of शशधर
4. न्यायसिद्धान्तमुक्तावली[6] of विश्वनाथपञ्चानन

5. परामर्श प्रकरणम् (अनुमानचिन्तामणि) of गंगेश उपाध्याय

Among the above-mentioned Sanskrit original works the text of *Śaśadhara* i.e. NSD was found to be a complete work with this regard. Here, he presents the objections raised by opponents systematically, refutes it and finally gives his own view at the end.

Now let us cast our look into the gallery of modern works on *parāmarśa.* The list follows like this :

1. Aruna chakraborty: न्यायदर्शने परामर्श *(Bengali),* Calcutta, 1978.
2. S.C. Chartterjee: *Nyāya* theory of knowledge, pp 261-265.
3. S.S. Barlingay: A modern introduction to Indian logic, Delhi, 1965, pp. 112-119
4. K.H. Kulkarni: *parāmarśa* in *Navya-Nyāya* (PhD. Dissertation), CASS, University of Pune.
5. Baliram *Śukla:* अनुमान प्रमाण *(Hindi),* Eastern Book Linkers, 1986.
6. Gopinatha Bhattacharya explains the 'controversy regarding *parāmarśa*' while editing *Tarkasamgraha,* Calcutta, 1976, pp. 188-189.
7. L.C. Mullatti: The *Navya-Nyāya* theory of inference, Dharwad, 1977, pp. 85-87
8. Yasumoto, T. : *Liṅgaparāmarśa* in *Nyāyavārttika*[7].
9. Karl H. Potter : Encyclopedia of Indian philosophies, 1977, pp. 188-189.
10. S.C. *Vidyābhūṣaṇa:* History of Indian logic, Calcutta, 1978, pp. 433-434, 510.
11. D.C. Guha: *Navya-Nyāya* system of logic, Delhi, 1979.

**These works do not meet the contemporary challenges**

The survey of these works does not meet the contemporary challenge. They all have emphasized on the nature and function of *parāmarśa.* Very few of them have adopted a right approach to the problem. However, Mrs. Anuna Chakraborty's work, in this connection, can be considered. Here, she devoted a full chapter under the title *'parāmarśer anumitikārṇatā',* where she presents the objections raised by *Mīmāṃsakas* following the chapter *'parāmarśa prakaraṇa'* of *Gangesa.* It is observed that this chapter does not cover a wider area i.e. some *Nyāya* based discussions are there. Dr. Mullatti presents a clear picture of inference and the component involved therein but does not go deep to discuss the problem while explaining *parāmarśa.* Dr. *Vidyābhūṣaṇa* has presented a summary of *parāmarśa* while he translates *'parāmarśa prakarṇa',* but is not enough to analyze the problem. Dr. *Śukla* though presents a clear picture of the process with its components still he has not put much emphasis on the controversy. Therefore, the works are felt to be inadequate, because they do not throw much light on the challenging discussions of *parāmarśa.*

**Scope of present work**

The present study, therefore, is an attempt to fill such gap. The whole study is based upon the text *liṅgaparāmarśa-vāda* of *Śaśadhara,* were the objections of opponents have been identified and have been solved from every possible angle. The summary of present study can be presented in the following manner : there are two parts of this work. Part one covers nine chapters such as :

**A brief discussion of the process of Inference : First chapter**

Before entering into the philosophical discussions of

*parāmarśa* it is felt to be necessary to know the process of inference in various systems. The quarries like 'What is their standpoint?' 'Do they need *parāmarśa* or not?' and 'What is the method they follow?' have been discussed here. Keeping all these points ahead this chapter has been formatted. This chapter presents the entire process of Inference as it occurs in *Nyāya* and other philosophical systems with its varieties such as: What is Inference? How does it occur? And what are its varieties?

**Components involved in the process of Inference : Second Chapter**

From the analysis of the process of inference we find components like *pakṣa, sādhya, vyāpti, parāmarśa, pakṣa-dharamatā,* etc., which are involved in the process. Unless we know the nature and function of these components we won't be able to explain inference. This chapter is an attempt to identify various components involved in the process of Inference and their natures and functions.

**Theory of Inference according to the *Mimāṁsakas* : Third Chapter**

Without knowing the military strategy of opponents no worrier will proceed to fight. Similarly, before proceeding to the battlefield in the form of philosophical discussions it is necessary to study the standpoints of opponents throughly. Keeping this in mind third chapter has been designed. Here, the *Mimāṃsā* account of Inference has been presented. While doing so, an attempt has been made to present in clear terms to the process of Inferential cognition as accepted in the system of *Mimāṃsā*. Here too, I have identified the elements involved in the entire process of Inference.

**Theory of Inference according to *Prācīna-nyāya* : Fourth chapter**

Logic differs from logician to logician. Necessity brings

modification. A similar case has occurred in the *Nyāya* system. Starting from Gautama to Udayana the process of inference keeps on changing. For example, Gautama and *Vātsyāyanā* do not require *parāmarśa* whereas Udyotakara finds its application. On the other hand, *Jayanta Bhaṭṭa* is not ready to accept Udyotakara. In this way they differ from each other on the basis of their application. Unless we know their views perfectly we won't be able to present their opinions. That's why a complete survey of discussions right from Gautama up to Udayana on Inference has been presented here and Jayanta's views have been taken into consideration.

**Theory of Inference according to *Navya-nyāya* : Fifth chapter**

The concept may be same to all logicians but the method of application will be different. A similar case occurs in the *Nyāya* system. Old logicians' *(prācīna Naiyāyikas)* definitions were severely criticized by Buddhist logicians. Some logicians tried to redefine it and put it in a new shape. This is the new tradition of *Nyāya* system, which slightly differs from old logicians so far the modification is concerned. Here, the theory of Inference, as developed by *Navya-Nyāya,* has been presented. For this the text of *Śaśadhara, Gaṅgeśa* and others has been used as source books.

**The concept of *Tṛtīyaliṅgaparāmarśa* and its necessity : Sixth chapter**

After listening the word *Tṛtīyaliṅgaparāmarśa* a doubt may arise in mind like 'Is it different from *liṅgaparāmarśa*?' 'What is *parāmarśa* then?' To surf this doubt, in this chapter I have analyzed the meaning and function of these concepts. However, after making the concept *Tṛtīyaliṅgaparāmarśa* clear, the function of this concept has been discussed in this clapter.

**Objection raised against *Tṛtīyaliṅgaparāmarśa* : Seventh Chapter**

On what basis the opponents have raised the objections. What exactly they want to point out? And what is their standpoint? This chapter attempts to identify the ground, purpose and clarification of such points. To do so, this chapter has tried to collect all the views of *Mimāṁsakas* regarding *parāmarśa* and has identified their grounds.

***Śaśadhara's* reply to the objections : Eighth chapter**

This chapter aims to explain the replies made by *Śaśadhara*. Therefore, each objection, made by opponents, has been taken up and its reply has been presented in this chapter. To do so, the dialogue between the *Mimāṁsākas* and the *Navya Naiyāyikas* has been presented here.

**Conclusion : Conclusive chapter**

The entire dialogue has been critically examined and relevant conclusions has been drawn in this chapter. Here *Śaśadhara* presents the view of *Navya Naiyāyikas*.

At the end of the discussion this has been concluded that without this component i.e. *parāmarśa* a valid inferential cognition cannot be drawn.

Apart from this, in the introduction I have attempted to trace back the origin and development of the concept. A glimpse has been casted to various systems of Indian philosophy to find out the position of *parāmarśa*. For this I have used original Sanskrit texts so far available to me.

Part two of the work contains the Sanskrit text of *liṅgaparāmarśavāda* of *Śaśadhara* with English translation and explanatory notes. A descriptive bibliography and indices of important terms have followed this.

## Origin and development of the concept

Now let us discuss 'how the concept developed in Indian philosophy, especially in *Nyāya* system?'. The source book of this system is *Nyāyasūtra* composed by Gautama. He just mentions the names of four instruments of valid knowledge and gives the divisions of inference, the most important source of knowing. Nothing has been mentioned about *parāmarśa*. The next illuminating work of this system is the commentary of *Vātsyāyana* on *Nyāyasūtra*. He, while analyzing the term *'tatpurvaka'*, highlights three things such as:

(1) perception of the relation of probans with that of probandum[8].

(2) remembrance of invariable concomitance[9] and

(3) remembrance of the relation is the cause of inferential cognition[10].

The above explanation of the commentator clearly states that *parāmarśa* is not involved in the process of inference. Of course, some modern writers opine that 'though the commentator has not mentioned *parāmarśa* clearly still it is understood from his explanation'[11].

Next comes Udyotakara, the celebrated logician of this school. He writes a sub-commentary on *Nyāyabhāṣya*. Here, we find the origin of the concept. In other words, he earns the credit of introducing this concept to the system[12]. He defines it like this: the pervader and pervaded (say, smoke and fire) are necessary components of producing the inferential cognition. The smoke is perveded by fire. This is called the rule of co-located-ness *(sahacāra niyama)* i.e. *vyāpti*. This happens in a *sapakṣa* i.e. kitchen etc. Later on if a qualified smoke *(viśiṣṭa dhūma)* will be perceived, the previous knowledge of invariable concomitance (of *hetu* and *sādhya)*, acquired from kitchen etc., will be recollected. Then the knowledge like *'vahnivyāpyadhūmavān ayam'* will arise. This is ealled *liṅgaparāmarśa*[13]. This knowledge of *parāmarśa*, according to Udotakara, is the cause of *amuniti* because immediately after that the knowledge of inferential cognition arises[14]. However, he has not given any definition of *parāmarśa* throughout the discussion.

Next logician of the system, following Udyotakara, is *Vācaspati Miśra*. He writes a commentary on *Nyāyavārttika*. Here he gives the definition of *parāmarśa*[15]. However, this definition of *Vācaspati Miśra* continued to exist. The later logicians developed the concept without defining it further. *Ācārya Jayantabhaṭṭa* does not accept this concept as a component of inferential cognition.

The concept of *parāmarśa* covered more pages when the new logicians tried to shape it in a different way. *Gaṅgeśa Upādhyāya* and the commentators of his work divided *parāmarśa* in the following way

क. प्रत्यक्षात्मक परामर्श[16]
अनुमित्यात्मक परामर्श
शब्दवोधात्मक परामर्श

ख. स्मरणात्मक परामर्श
अन्वयी परामर्श
व्यतिरेकी परामर्श

ग. व्याप्तिविशेष्यक परामर्श
पक्षविशेष्यक परामर्श

This, in short, is the origin and development of the concept.

**_Parāmarśa_ as in other systems**

Other logicians of various systems also have discussed the concept of *parāmarśa*. 'Ancient Buddhist logicians have used this word in the sense of 'purity and religious practices'[17]. In *Nyāyabinduṭikā* of same system it has been used as a 'referential cognition'[18]. We have also reference of *Jaina* logicians using this concept under the meaning of 'recollection'[19]. *Mīmāṁsā* system of Indian philosophy has used it as a component of inferential cognition i.e. 'confirmatory cognition'[20]. We find the usage of *parāmarśa* in *Bhāṭṭdīpīkā* of *Mīmāṁsd* system as a factor of causing remembrance[21]. *Ślokavārttika* has given the meaning as consideration[22]. *Nyāyakandali,* a *Vaiśeṣika* text, gives the meaning of *parāmarśa* as a 'subsumptive knowledge of a reason as abiding in the subject and as pervaded by the probandum.[23]

## FOOTNOTES

1. BP, verse- 66 व्यापारस्तु परामर्शः, करणं व्याप्तिधीर्भवेत्।
2. TCA-व्याप्तिविशिष्ट पक्षधर्मताज्ञानजन्यं ज्ञातं अनुमितिः।
3. This is *Mīmāṁsaks'* standpoint.
   तथाहि–प्रथमं व्याप्तेः स्मरणमनुभवो वा अनन्तरं व्याप्यत्वावच्छेदकधूमत्वादि धूम प्रकारकपक्षनिष्ठधूमज्ञानम्। अनन्तरमव्यवहितसमय एवानुमितिरप्रत्युहमुत्पद्यत एवेति। एवमप्युपपत्तौ अन्तरा विशिष्टज्ञानकल्पने तत्कारणत्वे च गौरवमेव बाधकम्। NSD, lpv.
4. तस्मात् सर्वथानुपपन्नो लिङ्गपरामर्शस्य चरमकारणताभिमानो नैयायिक....। Ibid.
5. I collected this manuscript from *Ānandāsrama,* Pune. unfortunately the colophon of this manuscript has been destroyed. The present incomplete manuscript contains 36 folios. It starts like this:
   श्री गणेशाय नमः।। वह्निव्याप्य धूमवान् पर्वत इति परामर्शाद् वह्निव्याप्य धूमवान् पर्वतो वह्निवान् इत्यादि अनुमित्याचार्या (?)।। तेषामयमाशयः।। तथाविधपरामर्शा-तादृशानुमितित्यनंगीकारे वह्निव्याप्यालोकवान्पर्वतइत्यादि परामर्शादपि विशेष्यक पर्वतोवह्निमानित्यनुमित्युत्पत्यापर्वतोद्येश्यक वह्नि विधेयकानुमितिं प्रति वह्निव्याप्य धूमप्रकारक पर्वत विशेष्यक। परामर्शस्य हेतुतायां व्यभिचारः तद्वारणार्थं धूमपरामर्श-जन्यतावच्छेदककादौस्वाप्तवह्नितोत्तररक्षणत्पत्तिकत्वादि सम्बन्धेन धूमपरामर्शवत्व निवेशनमावश्यकं (?) चिन्तामणिकार मते आचार्यमतः तु तादृशापरामर्शात्तथाविधानु-मिति अभ्युपगमे वह्निव्याप्यधूमप्रकारक पर्वतोद्देश्यक वह्निविधेयक अनुमितिं प्रति

वह्निव्याप्य धमूप्रकारक पर्वतविशेष्यक परामर्शविशेष्यक परामर्शत्वेन हेतुतायाः कल्पनीय......॥

6. Discussion based on verse no 67-68.
7. Journal of Indian and Buddhist Studies, University of Tokyo, Vol. VI, No-2, March 1958.
8. NBh. 1.1.5. तत्पूर्वकमित्यनेन लिङ्गलिङ्गिनोः सम्बन्धदर्शन चाभिसम्बध्यते।
9. Ibid. लिङ्गलिङ्गिनो सम्बन्धदर्शनेन लिङ्गस्मृतिरभिसम्बध्यते।
10. Ibid. स्मृत्या सम्बन्धदर्शनेन वाऽप्रत्यक्षोऽर्थोऽनुमीयते।
11. *Nyāya Darśane Parāmarśa,* Aruna Chakravorty, Calcutta. p. introduction:"- 'ख्'
12. N.V. 1.1.5 तदिदमन्तिमं प्रत्यक्षं पूर्वाभ्यां प्रत्यक्ष्याभ्यां स्मृत्या गृह्यमाणं परामर्शरूपमनुमानं भवति।
13. Ibid
14. Ibid.
15. Vide fourth chapter
16. NDP, introduction.
17. ...न परामर्शौ ...शुद्धयग्रभावतः–अभिधर्मकोश V.16.
18. तेषामेवाभिन्नायामप्यनुभवतारेण विजातीय व्यावृत्ततय प्रकृत्यैवैकार परामर्श प्रत्यय हेतुत्वात्–हेतुविन्दुटीका P.22
19. प्रमाणमवृत्तरुत्तकालभावी परामर्शत्वात्-स्यादवादमञ्जरी, 28
20. व्याप्तिविशिष्ट पक्षधर्मतात्मकम्–भाट्टचिन्तामणि–28, 30 (1.1.8)
21. तच्छब्दवलेन पूर्वोपकृतानामेव परामर्शात्–भाट्टदीपिका—4, 1cd, 3 (11.2.12)
22. यो.... दृश्यते परामर्शोऽर्थरूपस्य स कथं वोपद्यते–श्लोकवार्त्तिक 7-28
23. क्षणिकाश्रयं सत्वमित्यन्वयसिद्धिरिति चेत् न तावदर्थादिति सत्वस्य हेतोः परामर्श।–न्यायकन्दली 76.5

# PART - I

अनुमानापलापे तु प्रत्यक्षादपि दुर्लभा।
लोकयात्रेति लोकाः स्युः लिखिता इव निश्चलाः॥

—न्यायमञ्जरी, २१०

(If validity is denied to inference then all worldly transactions cannot be conducted with the mere help of perception. All the people of the world will become motionless as if they are painted in a picture).

## CHAPTER - I

# A BRIEF DISCUSSION OF THE PROCESS OF INFERENCE

### General Background

The cause of all human behavior is knowledge[1]. Knowledge of the objects of the Universe. Without this the human being won't be able to behave consistently with the world. Again, this knowledge is of two kinds viz. true or valid and false or invalid. False or invalid knowledge gives birth to a false experience, which goes against human behavior. Which does not represent the real nature of its object. What remains is a valid knowledge. Now, a problem arises that how to distinguish a valid knowledge from an invalid one? What are the means over there through which we will come to know the real nature of an object? This problem creates a room for the intellectual traditions of Indian Philosophy to say something. It is accepted by all the traditional systems of Indian Philosophy that the knowledge, which is a very cause of human behavior, can be obtained either directly or indirectly. But these philosophical systems have a disagreement regarding the means or proofs of obtaining the knowledge. The number of proofs has varied greatly with different schools from one to eight.

This idea is as old as *Veda*. The *Vedic* seers also have realized the same. A historical study of inference provides some adequate information about the consciousness of the distinction of direct and indirect knowledge of *Ṛgvedic period.*

### *Anumāna,* a historical retrospection

In Prof. Jwala Prasad's language "the earliest text which appears to be significant for any inquiry are some verses in *Ṛgveda*[2].

A study of these, as will be shown presently, indicates on the part of their authors a consciousness of the following facts: (i) those that are immediately present to the senses; and (ii) those are not immediately present to the senses, that is to say, those that are remote[3]....." In short, it can be concluded that, the seers understood the cause of the Universe by means of reflection, and have been inferred through another means of knowing about the things, which are remote. *Upaniṣadas (Jājñavalkya,* 3-7) and *Āraṇyakas*[4], in this regard, are in no way exceptional.

### *Anumāna* as in *Nyāya*

Now let us discuss that how the Indian philosophical systems have developed this idea in the later period. *Nyāya-Vaiśeṣika* school of Indian Philosophy accepts four means of obtaining knowledge. In philosophical terminology these ways of knowing are called *pramāṇas.* It is called *pramāṇa* because it maps the reality of the knowledge.

Therefore, these are considered as the instruments of obtaining a valid knowledge[5]. *Pramāṇa* has a real correspondence with objects, in the sense that the nature and attributes of the objects, as revealed by *Pramāṇas,* are not contradictory, despite of all variations in time, place and other conditions[6].

### What is Inference?

Those four proofs or means are perception, inference, comparison and verbal testimony[7], which generate different kinds of valid knowledge. *Anumāna* or inference is an important source of knowledge. This is the instrument of inferential cognition. The word *Anumana* is a kind of knowledge *(māna),* which we get after *(anu)* some other knowledge[9]. So, the after knowledge of an object or the probandum *(liṅgi, artha)* through a probans *(liṅga)* is called inference. The word *'anu'* conveys that this knowledge is followed by some other knowledge. In other words, it is a dependent knowledge. It is dependent on perception, which is an immediate knowledge. *Vātsyāyana* holds that "no inference can follow in the absence of perception"[10].

**Definition of inference**

The definition of *anumāna* has been discussed in an ascending manner starting from *Gotama* to *Gangeśa.* According to *Gotama* that is called inference, which is preceded by it, is of three kinds, namely, *pūrvavat, ṣeśavat* and *sāmānyatodṛṣṭa*[11]. Here the paraphrase 'preceded by it' is not so clear. Immediately after that *Vātsāyana,* the commentator of *Nyāyasūtra,* explains the word saying 'the perception of the (invariable) relation between the probans and the probandum as well as 'the perception of the probans'. The perception of the invariably related probans and probandum means the recollection of the probans. Through this recollection and perception of the probans the object will be inferred which is not a direct knowledge[12].

'What is the necessity of accepting inference, only one proof or means of obtaining valid knowledge i.e. perception can fulfill all the requirements' is the objection raised by *Chārvāk* philosophers[13]. This is the only school, which does not accept inference and at the same time asks for the ground of its establishment.

*Vācaspati Miśra,* a prominent scholar of *Nyāya* tradition with other philosophers, prepares a ground to establish the validity of inference[14]. The whole thing is in a dialogue from such as:

**Ground of establishing inference**

*Chārvākas :* Only perception is enough. We don't accept another *pramāṇa* called Inference?

*Naiyāyikas:* Well, it's up to you.

*Chārvākas:* But why you people accept it? What is the ground there?

*Naiyāyikas:* By the way, why do you ask this question to the people like us? Why not to anybody else?

*Chārvākas:* Because you people accept it.

*Naiyāyikas:* You mean to say that we have either doubt or illusion in our mind and you want to remove it.

*Chārvākas:* Right.

*Naiyāyikas:* But how did you come to know that? What is the instrument with you, through which you measure the ignorance, and doubt or illusion lies in others? Can you perceive that doubt etc. directly?

*Chārvākas:* No, this is the speech of a person, which proves the entire thing.

*Naiyāyikas:* Right, this the ground. Through the speech only we come to know the mental condition of a person. This works as a mark or sign and this is nothing but inference.

Thus, they establish the validity of inference.

**How does it occur?**

The *Nyāya-Vaiśeṣika* system of Indian philosophy has developed a systematic process of inference. This process consists of a number of components, which are related altogether in a particular way. The *Nyāya* system analyses the process of inference like this: A person, bearing the knowledge of invariable concomitance *(vyāpti)*[15] of smoke and fire in his mind, sees the smoke on the mountain. Just after the perception of the smoke on the mountain he recollects that smoke is invariably associated with fire. Immediately after that the knowledge like 'the mountain is possessed of smoke which is pervaded by fire' arises. This is called *Parāmarśa*. After the knowledge of *Parāmarśa* there arises the knowledge like 'the mountain possess fire'. This is called inferential cognition. The above process of inference can be explained like this:

The process so far

1) *hetu darśan* (perception of *hetu* or sign on the *pakṣa).*
2) *vyāpti smaraṇa* (remembrance of invariable concomitance between probans and the probandum).
3) *parāmarśa*—( that the *pakṣa* possesses *hetu* which is pervaded by *sādhya).*
4) *anumiti* - ( inferential cognition or the result)

This is the process of inference in short.

In *Nyāya* system the classifications of inference are seen in various forms. It is classified on the basis of both psychological and logical grounds. All and above there are three main classifications of inference[16].

**The Varieties**

Psychologically, it is of two kinds, viz. *Svārtha* (for one's sake) and *parārtha* (for the sake of others). And on the basis of logic it is said to be of three kinds. According to *Prācīna Nyāya,* there are three types of inference like: *pūrvavat, śeṣavat* and *sāmānyatodṛṭa* whereas; *Navya-Nyāya* classifies inference like *kevalānvayi, kevala-vyatireki* and *anvaya-vyatireki*. Let us discuss these three classifications of inference elaborately.

### First type of the classifications

The first type of classification puts inference into two, namely, *svārtha* and *parārtha*. This division of inference is not available either in *Gotama sūtra* or in the *Vaiśeṣika sūtra* of *Kaṇāda*. It is *Praśastapāda*[17], who mentioned it for the first time in the commentary of *Vaiśeṣkasūtra*. This same classification is also seen in the later period of *Nyāya* School. It is *Udayanācārya* and *Jayanta Bhaṭṭa*[18], who have classified inference in this style. *Ācārya Udyotakara*[19], the sub-commentator of *Nyāyasūtra,* mentions a word like '*parapratipādika*' which proves the superiority of the tradition of accepting the division.

### Inference for one's sake

If a person wants to convince to himself and for that if he follows the process to infer something then that will be called as *svārthānumāna*[20]. For example, a person makes out a universal proposition *(vyāpti)* that 'where there is smoke there is fire' from repeated observations of smoke and fire in kitchen etc.

This universal proposition is nothing else than a relation between two things and is called invariable concomitance. Bearing this knowledge in his mind, one day he happens to see a string of smoke somewhere on the mountain *(hetu darśan)*. All of sudden he will remember the universal proposition of smoke and fire *(vyāpti smaraṇa)*. Then he will realize that this smoke, like that of kitchen, is also invariably associated with the fire *(parāmarśa)*. Then he will have the knowledge of inferential cognition of fire *(anumiti)*. This, in short, is called the inference for one's sake.

### Inference for other's sake

The inference for others is a demonstrative one. The

demonstration with the help of five membered syllogisms. A person, being convinced for himself, attempts to convince the same to others[21]. This is based on a pure psychology. For that he needs some formal statements. In short, the later one is totally dependent on the former one. Those syllogistic expressions or *avayavas* are: 1) proposition *(pratijñā),* 2) the reason *(hetu),* 3) the example *(udāharaṇa),* 4) the application *(upānaya)* and the conclusion *(nigamana)*. Such as:

Somebody proposes like 'the hill has fire' *(pratijñā)*

Because it has 'smoke' *(hetu)*

'Where there is smoke there is fire' for example, in a kitchen *(udāharaṇa)*

This 'smoke is also associated with fire' *(upanaya)*

Therefore, 'it has fire' *(nigamana)*

Here, *pratijñā* or assertion is a statement or proposition, which is to be inferred. This lets know to the hearer what exactly is going to be inferred. For example, the mountain is fiery. This statement is a proposition, because later it is going to be proved.

After having such statement, now the hearer proceeds to know that on what ground this statement is true. Then he is told that there is smoke. From the perception of smoke he can conclude that it is a valid assertion. This is called *hetu* or reason. This supplies a ground for the establishment of the above assertion.

An example *(udāharaṇa)* is a reminding factor of the relation of invadable concomitance between probans and the probandum. After seeing the smoke on the hill he recollects the similar instances, which he had experienced in the kitchen etc. This is called example, the third member of the syllogism.

*Upanaya* is the fourth member of the group. This consists

of two conditions like: there is smoke on the mountain *(pakṣadharmatājñāna)* and that smoke is invariable associated with fire *(vyāptijāna)*. Now the hearer combines these two into a complete one. And what he gets is *parāmarśa.*

The last member of that group is *nigamana* or conclusion. It declares what had been asserted to be such as: there is fire on the hill has been proved.

**Second type of the classifications**

According to second type of classification the inference is divided into three kinds such as : *pūrvavat, śeṣavat* and *sāmānyatodṛṣṭa*[22]. It is *Gotama,* who mentions these three forms of inference. After that *Vātsyāyana.* the commentator of *Nyāyasūtra,* comes forward to explain it in a systematic way. He has derived the meanings of the classification in two ways[23].

***Pūrvavat***

According to *Vātsyāyana* that is called *pūrvavat,* where the effect is inferred from its cause[24]. That means, a *pūrvavat* inference is that in which we infer the unperceived effect from a perceived cause. For example, we see the rising clouds in the sky and inferred that the rain is going to fall. It is an inference of some unknown thing (future rainfall) from a known thing (rising clouds). In short, *purvat* is known as *kāraṇa-liṅgaka.*

***Śeṣavat***

A *śeṣavat* type of inference is the just opposite to *pūrvavat*[5]. It is inferred through an unperceived cause from a perceived effect. For example, a past rainfall of a river is inferred from its fullness or muddiness of water, swiftness of current, which are perceived. This type of inference is known as *kārya-liṅgaka.*

***Sāmānyatodṛṣṭa***

*Sāmānyatodṛṣṭa* type of inference is the perception of some object at some time which was somewhere else due to its movement[26]. This inference is based on generalized relationship. For example, the movement of the sun. The motion of the sun cannot be perceived directly.

**Third type of the classifications**

The third type of classification is specially designed by new logicians[27]. But we find such division in *Nyāyavārtika* also. Here it explains the types with relevant examples. This division is based on different methods of establishing *vyāpti* or invariable concomitance. These are (1) *kevalānvayi,* (2) *kevalavyatireki* and (3) *anvayivyatirekin.*

This inference occurs when there is the relation of invariable concomitance between the subject and the object. Here the knowledge of invariable concomitance between probans and probandum is seen only through the methord of agreement in presence *(anvaya)*, since there is no negative instance of their agreement in absence.

***Kevalānvayi* (only positive)**

This will be applied there where the subject and object go together. For example,

> 'All knowable things are nameable
> pot is a knowable thing
> Therefore, it is nameable.'

In the above example, there is an affirmative concomitance between knowability and nameability. All things are knowable and nameable. We can't just find its negative concomitance.

***Kevalāvyatireki* (only negative)**

This inference is obtained only through the negative invariable concomitance. It is dependent on a *vyāpti* or invariable concomitance between major term with that of the middle term. In this case *vyāpti* is a purely negative proposition[29]. For instance, 'what is not different from other element has no smell

The Earth has smell

Therefore, the Earth is different from other elements.'

**Anvaya vyatireki (both positive and negative):**

This type of inference contains both positive and negative kind of invariable concomitance[30]. In other words, there is *vyāpti* or invariable concomitance between the presence of the middle term with the presence of major term as well as between the absence of the major term and absence of the middle term. For example, if somebody proposes a statement like "where there is smoke there is fire" will be true and the statement like "where there is no smoke there is no fire" is also true. The former is the example of positive concomitance whereas, the later one is the example of the negative one. Therefore, the statement like 'mountain possesses fire because of smoke' is the instance of both positive and negative invariable concomitance. In short, we will have a look over the varieties of the inference.

INFERENCE

↓

| ↓ | ↓ | ↓ |
|---|---|---|
| Classification on the basis of the purpose | Classification on the basis of the perceptibility | Classification on the basis of the *vyāpti* |
| ↓ | ↓ | ↓ |
| *Svārtha* | *Pūrvavat* | *Kevalānvayi* |
| ↓ | ↓ | ↓ |
| *Parārtha* | *Śeśavat* | *Kevalavyatireki* |
| | ↓ | ↓ |
| | *Sāmānyatodṛṣṭa* | *Anvayivyatireki* |

Though different opinions are observed between the two schools *(Navya nyāya* and *prācīna nyāya)* regarding the structure of inference still the function of both the divisions are same. The components, which are involved in the process of inference, will be discussed in the next chapter.

## Inference as in *Sāṃkhya*

After discussing the *Nyāya* theory of inference now I proceed to sketch a brief discussion of the process of inference as occurs in other philosophical systems. *Sāṃkhya* system considers inference as the knowledge of the pervader *(vyāpya)* arises from the knowledge of invariable concomitance[31]. And the result is the understanding of the concerned person[32]. *Sāṃkhya kārikā* explains inference as based upon the cognition of middle term and the major term[33]. According to this system inference is of three kinds such as: *pūrvavat, śeṣavat and sāmānyatoḍṛṣṭa*[34]. A further division of the inference is also available in this system like *vīta and avīta.* This system requires a ten-membered syllogism in the context of inference.

## *Vedāntic* concept of inference

*Saṃkarācārya,* the founder of *advaita vedānta,* holds that there is no necessity of inference with regard to trans-candal knowledge *(pāramārthikajñāna)* but it can be applied into the empirical world *(vyāvahārika jñāna*[35]). This school accepts Inference as instmment of inferential cognition. And inferential cognition is that which is generated by know-ledge of pervasion, functioning as cognition of pervasion.[36] *Medghanādasūri,* a great figure of *Viśiṭādvaitavedānta,* characterizes as two terms i.e. pervader and the perdaded having a positive invariable concomitance between them and from the sight of the pervaded the remote perveder's remembrance occurs[37]. *Madhācārya*, the founder of *Dvaitave-dānta,* defines inference as *'nirdoṣopapattiranumānaṃ.'*[38] Here, *upapatti* means *liṅga* or mark[39].

So, the faultless mark, qualified by invariable concomitance, is called inference. Here, there is a division of inference as *kāraṇānumāna, kāryānumāna and sāmānyānumāna*[40].

*Prasthānaratnākara,* a *suddhādvaita Vedāntins* text, defines inference as the instrument of inferential cognition. And inferential cognition is a product of an instrument namely invariable concomitance. However, this system accepts three membered-syllogism.

**The concept of inference in Jaina philosophy**

*Pramāṇa,* according to *Jaina* logicians, is *'svaparābhāsi'.* That means it is the knowledge, which reveals itself as well as to others without any hindrance. Basically, this system has a difference of opinions regarding the numbers of *pramāṇas.* Some Jaina logicians say it is two whereas, some other accepts it as four[40]. The definition of inference, as has been given by *jaina* ogicians, is *'anu'* means after and *'māna'* means the instrument through which the knower obtains the knowledge of place, time and nature[41]. *'Anu'* here indicates the remembrance of the knowledge of invariable concomitance between probans and probandum.

So, after perceiving smoke from a distance, the person remembers the invariable concomitance of probans and probandum and immediately after that the inferential cognition arises in him. The old *Jaina* logicians accept three types of inference whereas, the new logicians, accept two namely inference for one's self and inference for others sake[42].

*Jaina* logicians also accept *vyāpti* as a main part of the process of inference. It, according to them, is an invariable relationship of two objects. Further, they accept *vyāpti,* as of two kinds[43], like *anvayavyāpti and vyatirekavyāpti.* The components, which are engaged to produce inference, are *pakṣa, sādhya, vyāpti, hetu and hetvābhāsa.* The number of syllogisms varies here. Some say it is five whereas ten others.

The faults of inference are *pakṣābhāsa, hetvābhāsa* and *dṛṣṭāntābhāsa. Pakṣābhāsa* is of five kinds, *dṛṣṭāntābhāsas* are two in number and *hetvābhāsa,* according to Siddhasena Divākara, is of three kinds such as: *asiddha, viruddha and aneikāntika.*

This is the process of inference according to *Jaina* logicians.

**Inference according to Buddhist logicians**

The Buddhist School of Indian philosophy accepts *pramāṇa as infallible knowledge*[44] *(is the right cognition),* of two kinds because of two types of objects *(mānaṃ dvividhaṃ viṣayadvaividhyāt).* Logicians of this system hold that the objects can be perceived either directly or indirectly. No third alternative can be entertained. But we find the reference regarding four types of *pramāṇas* in *Pre-Dignāga* school of Buddhisim[45]. In Prof. Stcherbatsky's language[46], "the direct knowledge as has been defined by Buddhist logicians, is a synthesis between a sensation and a conception, the indirect one is a synthesis between a sensation and two concepts". Buddhist logicians hold *pramā* as practically useful knowledge and *pramāṇa* is its source. Hence, *pramāṇa* has a capacity to reveal the real nature of the objects.

This revelation can be obtained either directly or indirectly. Therefore, this system holds only two *pramāṇas* viz. Perception and inference as two different sources of acquiring the real nature of the objects.

**The definition**

Inference, according to this school, is cognition of an object through its mark. They hold mark as a possessor of three qualities viz. its presence in the subject, its presence in similar instances and its presence in dissimilar instances. So, the inference is a knowledge of an object through a mark, which (mark) possesses the above three aspects[47]. Buddhist logicians classify inference as *svārtha*(inference for one self) and *parārtha* (inference for other's sake).

**Svārthānumāna**

Inference for one self is a knowledge of an object through its mark. In other words, the cognition of *sādhya* arises in a person who happens to see the reason[48]. The inference for other's sake, according to Dignāga, has three elements viz. *Pakṣa, hetu and dṛṣṭānta.* He, otherwise, calls it *sādhana*[48]. If any element of these three happens to be defective then the total inference will be defective. According to him, there are three types of *sādhanābhāsas (*fallacious grounds*)* namely, *pakṣābhāsa (*fallacious grounds*), hetvābhāsa* (fallacious reasons) and *dṛṣṭāntābhāsa* fallacious examples.[49]

Thus, the process of inference for others occurs when a reason is set to produce a conviction in others. Here, Buddhist logicians have employed three syllogisms or *nyāyāvayavas* like an inferential subject, a probandum and an examples[50]. This syllogism is a cause which produces an inference. *Nyāyabindu* explains syllogism concedes in communicating the three aspects of the logical mark for others. Out of these three components they form a reasoning.

That is like this;

| | |
|---|---|
| The proposition: | This mountain is fiery |
| The reason: | Because it has smoke |
| The example: | All that has smoke is fiery like kitchen and Whatever is not fiery has no smoke like lake etc[51]. |

**Components of inference : Vyāpti**

There are two main components of inference as it occurs in Budhhist logic. The first one is *Vyāpti* or invariable concomitance and the second is *Pakṣadharmatā*. The former is the ground of establishing inference whereas the latter is a supporter of that ground. Invariable concomitance as discussed in *Pramāṇavārtika* is like this. The *vyāpti* is not the mere observation of some positive instance of a particular relation, for example, between smoke and fire[52]. This case, according to Buddhist logicians, is not enough to establish the relationship between smoke and fire because the observation proves that they were connected in the past. This cannot satisfy the entire case. On the other hand, it cannot be dependant on some negative instances of fire and smoke because we cannot assure that there will be no instances in future of the presence of smoke in the absence of fire.

Therefore, the *vyāpti* is proved neither by perception nor by non-perception. But by the knowledge of causality or identity. Instead of saying 'where there is smoke there is fire' we can say that 'smoke is produced when fire is produced. And it is not there where fire is not there'. So also in the case of identity. When it is known that 'A' possesses the nature of 'B' then we can define such types of relationship there. Because in this case, without one the other cannot exist. This *Vyāpti* is of two kinds such as: *Anvaya* and *Vyatireka*.

**Pakṣadharmatā**

*Pakṣadharmatā* is another main component of the process of inference. A mere *hetu* having an invariable relationship with *sādhya* cannot produce a valid inference. *Pakṣadharmatā* is one of three forms of *hetu* which means *pakṣyesattvaṃ*. Another two types are like *pakṣyesatvaṃ* (the presence of probans in similar instances) and *vipakṣeasavttaṃ* (the absence of probans in dissimilar instances). According to Budhhist logicians, the *hetu* is of three kinds such as *Kārya, Svabhāva* and *Anupalambha*. The first one shows the cause and effect relationship like where there is smoke there is fire whereas the second one proclaims the identity.

## Faults of inference

In the above example the mountain is an inferential subject. If in any case it happens to be proved as false then the inference will be false. In the similar way, a false probandum and example will draw a wrong conclusion. Therefore, Buddhist logicians have identified three kinds of defective grounds *(sādhanābhāsas),* of which a fallacious subject *(pakṣābhāsa)* comes first.

## Paksābhāsa

*Ācārya Dignāga* has mentioned four types of fallacious subjects[53] viz.

1. A fallacious ground against perception, *(Pratyakṣa-viruddha)*
2. An inferential ground against inference *(Annumāna-viruddha)*
3. An inferential ground denying the synonyms *(Pratiti-viruddha)*
4. An inferential ground against one's own belief *(Svava-canaviruddha)*

The first one, for instance "sound is inaudible", goes against our perception.

And if such fallacious ground happens to be an inferential subject then it will give birth to a false inference. The second type goes against our experience. For example, " a pot is eternal". In fact, it is not so because it is a product and products are non-eternal.

The third type of fallacious ground denies the similarities. Like when somebody says, "the moon is not *candra*". And the fourth one goes against one's own statement like "Inference is not a source of knowledge". However, Dignāga in his treatise called *Nyāyapraveśa* has mentioned nine types of fallacious grounds[54].

**Hetvābhāsas**

Fallacious reasons, according to Dignāga[55], is of three kinds such as: *asiddha* (the unproved), *aneikāntika (the inconclusive)* and *bādhita* (the contradictory one). Again, he subdivides *asiddha* into four, *aneikāntika* into six and *bādhita* into four. So, the total number is fourteen whereas, *Ācārya Dharmakīrti*[56] gives the total number as eight.

**1. Asiddha :**

*Dignāga* does not give any definition of *asiddha.* He only mentions its categories. But as its name suggests this reason is not proved. There are four divisions such as:

(a) *Ubhayāsiddha:* this kind of fallacious reason is unacceptable as a predicate to both the parties i.e. two systems. For example, Sound is non-eternal, because it is visible.

(b) *Anyatarāsiddha :* It is acceptable by one party only i.e. by either system. For example,

Sound is evolved

Because it is a product.

Here, according to *Mīmāṃsakas* and *Sāṃkhya* philosophers, *Śabda* or word cannot be manifested but it can be created.

(c) *Saṃdigdhāsiddha :* this type of fallacious reason has a doubtful existence. For example,

The hill is fiery,

Because there is vapour,

Here mist can be mistaken as smoke.

(d) *Āśrayāsiddha :* here its very existence is doubtful. For example,

Ether is a substance

Because it has qualities.

**2. *Aneikāntika :***

Again, *aneikāntika* is of six kinds:

**a. *Sādhāraṇa Aneikāntika:***

*Aneikāntika* : here the middle term is too common, it resides in the major term as well as in the opposite of it. For example,

Sound is eternal

Because, it is knowable (i.e. knowable can be eternal things as well as non-eternal things).

**b. *Asādhārana Aneikāntika:***

Sound is eternal

because it is audible

Here, *Śravaṇatva* is an uncommon thing. It exists neither in the major term nor in its opposite.

**c. *Sapakṣaikadeśavṛittirvipakṣvyāpī aneikāntika:***

It resides in some similar instances but does not reside in all the dissimilar instances. For example,

Sound is not a product of effort

because it is non-eternal

**d. *Vipakṣaikadeśavṛttiḥ sapakṣvyāpī aneikāntika:***

It resides in some unlike instances but in all like instances. For example,

Sound is a product of effort

Because it is non-eternal.

**e. *Ubhayapakṣaikadeśavṛtti aneikāntika:***

This type of fallacious reason resides only in a part of similar instance and that of dissimilar instances as well.

Sound is eternal

Because it is incorporeal

**f. *Viruddhābhicāri aneikāntika:***

That which has a contradictory invariable concomitance.[57]

Sound is non-eternal

Because it is a product

Here, the invariable concomitance is 'whatever is non-eternal is a product, like pot' *(Vaiśeṣika opines)* and

Sound is eternal

Because it is always audible

Here, the invariable concomitance is 'whatever is eternal is audible, like sound etc.' *(Mimāṃāsakas* opine like this).

Here, both the reasonings are correct, but this leads to a contradictory conclusion.

**3. Biruddha :**

It is again of four kinds such as :

(a) *Dharmasvarūpaviparītasādhana:* that which proves the very opposite nature of the thing that which is going to be proved.

Sound is eternal

Because it is a product

(b) *Dharmaviśeṣa viparītasādhana:* here, the *sādhana* or *hetu* itself is contradictory to the major term. For example,

The eye etc. are in service of somebody else

Because, these are made out of particles, like bed etc.

(c) *Dharmisvarūpaviparītasādhana:* It occurs when the middle term is inconsistant with the minor term. For example[58],

*Sāmānya* is neither a substance nor a quality, nor an action.

Because, it depends upon one substance and possessed qualities and action, like generality-particularity. But in fact, generality does not depend upon particularity.

(d) *Dharmiviśeṣaviparītasādhana:* That which proves the opposite of the particular kind of *Dharmin* that means probandum is called *Dharmiviśeṣaviparītasādhana.* In the above example the *bhāva* may not only a *dravya* or *guṇa* or *karma* but it may be *asatpratyayakartu* like *abhāva.*

**Dṛṣṭāntābhāsas:**

The number of fallacious examples varies among the Buddhist logicians. *Dignāga* mentions the number as ten whereas, *Achārya Dharmakīrti* extends the number up to eighteen. However, they have divided the fallacious examples into two categories like heterogeneous fallacies *(Vaidharmya Dṛṣṭāntābhāsas)* and homogeneous fallacies *(Sādharmya Dṛṣṭāntābhāsas).* Both the types have equal numbers i.e. each class has some sub types. Here, my discussion is based upon *Dignāga's Nyāyapraveśa*[59].

*(a) Sādhanāsiddha:* An example non-cooperating with the thing that which helps to establish probandum. For example,

Sound is eternal

Because it is incorporeal *(amūrta)*

That which is incorporeal is eternal, like an atom.

Here the example i.e. atom cannot serve the purpose because they are not incorporeal by nature.

*(b) Sādhyadharmāsiddha:* An example non-cooperating with that, which is going to be proved (the probandum). For example,

Sound is eternal

Because it is incorporeal

That which is incorporeal is eternal like intelligence.

The intelligence is the example here, which is not eternal. So, this also is not able to serve the purpose.

*(c) Ubhayāsiddha:* An example which is neither co-operative with middle term nor with the major term. For example,

Sound is eternal

Because it is incorporeal

That which is incorporeal is eternal, as a pot

*(d) Ananvaya:* An example showing lack of universal connection between probans and probandum. For example,

This pot is eternal

Because it is a product

That which is a product is eternal like a cloth.

*(e) Viparitānvaya:* Here, this example shows a reverse invariable concomitance between middle term and major term. For example, "here it is seen that which is a product is eternal". The invariable concomitance will be like whatever is non-eternal is a product, like pot etc. It goes against our experience.

Similarly, heterogeneous examples also do not serve the purpose. He has mentioned five kinds of heterogeneous examples with their respective examples, such as:

*(f) Sādhyāvyāvṛtta* (non-existent of probandum)

*(g) Sādhanāvyāvṛtta* (non-existent of probans)

*(h) Ubhayāvyāvṛtta* (non-existent of both i.e. probans and probandum)

*(i) Avyatireka* (a heterogeneous example showing an absence of disconnection between probans and probandum)

*(j) Viparītavyatireka* (The case where the absence of probans and probandum is reversed).

## FOOTNOTES

1. सर्वव्यवहारहेतुर्बुद्धिर्ज्ञानम्, TSA
2. Important verses are 1.164.4 & 37, X.82.3 &4, X.129.6 & 7
3. HIE, p. 10
4. स्मृतिप्रत्यक्षैतिह्यं अनुमान चतुष्टयम्।–तैत्तरीयारण्यक, १.२
5. TSA
6. NVTT 1.1.1 as in NTK. P. 52
7. NS - 1.1.3
8. TSA
9. NBh. 1.1.3 मितेन लिङ्गेन लिङ्गिनोऽर्थस्यपश्चान्मानमनुमानम्।
10. NBh. 1.1.5
11. NS. 1.1.5
12. NBh. 1.1.5 तत्पूर्वकमित्यनेन लिङ्गलिङ्गिनोः सम्बन्धदर्शनं लिङ्गदर्शनं वाऽभिसम्बध्यते।
13. *Chārvāk* philosophers do not accept inference as a means of valid knowledge. According to them perception only can fulfill all the requirements.
14. Tarkabhāṣā, P-138, ed. by Surendradev Sastri
15. TSA
16. IL, p-162
17. PBh, *guṇe anumāna prakaraṇa* तस्मात्परार्थानुमानं वाक्योपपत्तेस्तदेकदेशा अवयवयुक्ता इति लक्षते।
18. NM, Ch. 2
19. NV 1.1.32, परप्रतिपादका ये वाक्याङ्गभूता इतरेतरा प्रत्ययितेनार्थवन्तो वाक्यांशतामुपयान्ति तेऽवयवाः।
20. TSA
21. TSA

22. NS 1.1.5
23. NBh 1.1.5, अथवा पूर्ववदिति...
24. Ibid
25. Ibid
26. Ibid
27. AC, *kevalānvayiprakaraṇa*
28. T.M., Ch. 2, यत्र साध्यव्यतिरेको न कुत्रपश्यति स केवलान्वयी।
29. Ibid, यत्र साध्यप्रसिद्धि पक्षातिरिक्ते नास्ति; स केवलव्यतिरेकि।
30. Ibid, यत्र साध्यं साध्याभावश्च अन्यत्र प्रसिद्धि सोऽन्वयव्यतिरेकि।
31. SS-1/100, प्रतिबद्धदृशः प्रतिबद्धज्ञानमनुमानम्।
32. *Bhāṣya on ibid,* अनुमितिस्तु पौरूषेय बोधः।
33. SK - 5
34. ibid
35. BSSB—2.1.11
36. *Vedāntaparibhāṣā,* ch. 2, गृहितान्वयोर्व्याप्यदर्शनात् परोक्षव्यापकावच्छेदक-ज्ञानमनुमानम्।
37. *Nayadyumaṇi,* p 195 as in BDB
38. *Daśaprakaraṇāni,* p - 34
39. ibid.
40. *Anumāna pramāṇa, p.* 235
41. *Syādbādamanjarī*-20, अनु पश्चाल्लिङ्गं सम्बन्ध ग्रहणानन्तर मीयते परिच्छिद्यते देशकालस्वभावविप्रकृष्टोर्थोनेन ज्ञानविशेषणं अनुमानम्।
42. *Anumāna pramāṇa, p.* 235
43. ibid, p. 214
44. NB, p. 4, अविसंवादकं ज्ञानं सम्यग्ज्ञानम्।
45. *Upāyahrudaya, p. 23 as in BDB, p.* 236, चतुर्विधं प्रमाणं प्रत्यक्षानुमान-मुपमानागमश्चेति।
46. BL, p. 231
47. NP, p. 7, अनुमानं लिङ्गार्थदर्शनम्। लिङ्गःपुनस्तिरूपमुक्तम्।
48. NB, Ch. 2
49. NP, p. 7, तत्र पक्षादि वचनानि साधनम्।

50. ibid.

51. According to Buddhist logicians *hetu* is of two kinds *sādhamya* and *vaidharmya*.

52. कार्यकारणभावाद् वा स्वाभावात् वा नियमकात्।
अविनाभावनियमोऽदर्शनान्न न दर्शनात्।। PV, 3-1

53 NB, Ch. 2

54. NP, Ch. 3

55. NP, p.2

56. ibid.

57. ibid.

58. ibid.

59. NP, p. 5

## CHAPTER-II

# COMPONENTS INVOLVED IN THE PROCESS OF INFERENCE

Components means any of the parts of which something is made. These components when they will be arranged in a systematic manner will build a large object. In other words, we can define a large object as a set of components, which are interrelated, which explain it fully, accurately and with a great care. Inference is a full process of knowing and a component means an element of that process.

**General background**

Now, let us assume inference as a large object to know its set of components. Inference is defined as the knowledge arising through *parāmarśa*[1]. What is *parāmarśa* then? *Parāmarśa* or confirmatory cognition is the knowledge of *pakṣadharmatā* qualified by the knowledge of invariable concomitance or *Vyāpti*[2]. Again, what is this *pakṣadharmatā? Pakṣadharmatā* is the presence of the probans in the inferential subject or *pakṣa*[3]. The invariable concomitance is the invariable association between probans and probandum.[4] So, we have components like *pakṣa, sādhya, vyāpti, parāmarśa, pakṣadharmata,* etc., which are involved in the process of inference. On the other hand, we can define or analyze inference through this set of components. Unless we know the nature and function of these components we won't be able to explain inference. Let us now discuss these terms one by one at length.

**Pakṣa : where presence of probandum is in doubt**

*Pakṣa* or subject is a substratum or locus, where the probandum is supposed to be established. This substratum may be a place, a substance, an individual or any other thing where an inferable thing can be predicted. The *pakṣa* is defined as the subject, in which the presence of probandum is in doubt[5]. Let us have the familiar example of the system: 'The mountain is fiery, because of smoke'. Here, fire is probandum, because it is going to be established. Smoke is the reason, because it helps probandum in its establishment. Somebody may start doubting regarding the existence of fire only after seeing smoke on the mountain. Hence, in this case the mountain performs the role of *pakṣa*. The word *pakṣa* is found, for the first time, in Gotama's *Nyāya-sūtra*[6]. But he means *pakṣa* as 'side' because in later *sūtras* he mentions terms like *svapakṣa, parapakṣa* etc. Next comes *Vātsyāyana,* he interprets *'pakṣa'* as 'establishing one's own thesis'. He also keeps the meaning 'side' unchanged. But it is *Udyotakara,* the sub-commentator of the *Nyāya-sūtra,* develops its meaning as 'the subject of proposition". Finally, that is called *pakṣa,* which possesses the property called *pakṣatā* or subjectness[8]. What is this *pakṣatā* then?

**Pakṣatā is the absence of certainty devoid of the desire to infer**

The word *pakṣatā* is derived from *pakṣa* with '*tal*' suffix, which represents the meanjng as 'the nature of *pakṣa* '. Every mountain cannot be a *pakṣa*. For that some necessary conditions are there. *Pakṣatā,* as it is defined by *Viśvanātha,* is the absence of certainty devoid of the desire to infer[9]. The mountain possessing the property called pakṣatā is called *pakṣa*[10]. Logicians define *pakṣatā* as where exists the absence of the knowledge of the probandum qualified by the absence of the desire to infer.[11] And that which possesses such quality is called *pakṣa*. The following four possibilities can occur in this case:

| | |
|---|---|
| + X -------> + Y | or both the entities i.e. probans and probandum are there in the *pakṣa*. |
| + X -------> - Y | or probans is there but no probandum is there in the *pakṣa*. |
| - X -------> + Y | or probans is not there but probandum is there in the *pakṣa* |
| - X -------> - Y | or both probans and probandum are not in the *pakṣa*. |
| -------------- | Here 'X' indicates 'probans' and 'Y' |
| -------------- | indicates 'Probandum' |

Among these possibilities in the last case there will be no inference, because both the components are absent there though there is a desire to establish the probandum.

**Pakṣadharmatā:**

The presence *of vyāpya* on the *pakṣa* or subject is ealled *Pakṣadharmatā*[12]. If this is the definition of *Pakṣadharmatā* then question may arise like 'why smoke alone is called *Pakṣ -adharm* ? Why not tree, stone etc. which are also there in *pakṣa?'* these are also property of mountain. The only possible answer for it is this that we do not infer fire on the basis of anything other than smoke. This is the only effective means. In other words, we can say that all smokes in the world, though they are pervaded by fire, are not the property of the inferential subject. So, in a palticular context a particular thing can become the property or *pakṣadharma*.

**_Pakṣadharmatā_, is the presence of _vyāpya_ on the _pakṣa_ or subject**

Again, *vyāpya* means that which is qualified by *vyāpti* or invariable concomitance. In other words, the presence of the reason on the subject, which (reason) is qualified by invariable concomitance, is known as *pakṣatā*. As mountain is the *pakṣa* in the inference, the cognition of 'smoke' as present in the *'pakṣa'* is the knowledge of *'vyāpya* 'as a property or *dharma* of that mountain. That's why it has been described as *pakṣadharmatā*. This with the help of some other things constitutes *parāmarśa*. That is to say that pakṣa is greatly dependent on *pakṣadharma*.

**_Sādhya_ : an inferable character of the subject of the inference.**

When a person sees smoke on the mountain, what he infers is 'either the hill is related to the fire' or 'fire is related to the hill'. From both the sentences he'll predict that 'some object' is on the mountain, which is invariably related to the smoke. And that is nothing but fire, because of his previous experience. *Sādhya* is the object of inference. It is said to be an inferable character of the subject of the inference. This *sādhya* is also called' *liṇgin'*, because it is related to *'liṇga'*[13] or mark. Again, it is known as *sādhya* because it is sought to be proved. It cannot be perceived directly but through its significant mark it is supposed to be inferred. For example, 'the mountain possesses fire, because of smoke'. Here, smoke is the indicator and what it indicates is fire, which is otherwise called *sādhya* or probandum.

**_Hetu_ is the means of establishing inference**

*Hetu,* as defined by *Gotama,* is the means for establishing what is to be established through the affirmative character of the example[14]. It is called '*hetu*' because it causes the knowledge of the probandum. It is the means of proving of the probandum, therefore, it is called instrument or *sādhana*. This also has termed as *'gamaka'* or indicator because it serves the purpose of indicating something (i.e. probandum). *Keśava Miśra*[15] derives the meaning of *liṅga* or mark as it is the perception of sign or mark which leads to the inference of probandum. For example, 'this mountain possesses fire, because it has smoke'. In this case, we assume to have fire on it, which can not be perceived directly. But it is smoke, which provides an adequate information for the same. It is stated before that *parāmarśa* or confirmatory cognition is a necessary condition for inference. And the definition of *parāmarśa* highlights the role played by *hetu* or probans to constitute it. Therefore, the classification of different kinds of *hetu* helps to understand different kinds of *vyāptijñāna* and *anumāna* as well. Keeping this view in mind, *Naiyāyikas* have categorized *hetu* in to three clases[16]. Let us discuss the nature and function of these categories.

**The varieties :**

**(a) *Anvayavyatireki liṅga***

If there is '+x' then there is '+y' *anvaya (yad satve yad sattvaṃ)* And if there is '-x' then there is '-y' *vyatireka (yadabhāve yadabhāvaṃ)*

Let us fit this in to the stock example of the system 'mountain possesses fire because of smoke'.

It can be shown like this:

where there is 'smoke' there is 'fire'—positive invariable con-comitance and where there is no 'fire' there is no 'smoke'— negative invariable concomitance.

So, the positive invariable concomitance occurs between presence of probans and probandum and the negative invariable concomitance occurs between the absence of probans and probandum. In short, the reason, which possesses both the type of invariable concomitance i.e. positive and negative, is called *anvayivyatireki hetu*.

**(b) *kevalānvayi***

The mark, which possesses only positive invariable concomitance between the probans and the probandum, is called *kevalānvayi* liṇga[17]. For example, 'the pot is nameable because it is knowable, like cloth etc.' Here, the reason or probans is knowability and the probandum is nameability and they pervade each other. In this case, only positive invariable concomitance i.e. where there is knowability there is nemability or vice-versa can be shown. So, the invariable concomitance is called *kevalānvayi* and since this mark possesses this type of invariable concomitance, it is called only positive mark.

**(c) *Kevala-vyatireki***

To clarify the term *kevalvyatireki* we can have an example like 'the earth is different from other than substances, because it has smell'. We cannot produce the negative invariable concomitance like 'where there is smell there is from other than substances'. Thus, the mark, which possesses the negative type of invariable concomitance, is called *kevala-vyatireki liṇga*[18].

***Sad-hetu* :**

**Characteristics of a sad-hetu**

Again, *hetu* can be either a *sad-hetu* or an *asad-hetu.* That is called a good reason or *sad-hetu,* which produces the true inferential cognition. Otherwise it will be called as a bad reason or an *asad-hutu*. A good reason has five characteristics like:

1) It must exist in the inferential subject *(pakṣe sattvaṃ)*

2) It should not be in similar instances *(sapakṣe asattvaṃ)*
3) It should not exist in the dissimilar instance *(vipakṣe asattvaṃ)*
4) It should not contradict *(abadhitatvaṃ)*
5) It should not have another reason to prove the opposite *(asatpratipakṣatvaṃ)*

If a reason is having such characteristics then it will be called a valid reason. It is a valid reason because it is capable of producing inference.

And that is called a bad reason, which appears as a *hetu* but is not a *hetu* in fact. This is technically called hetvābhāsa, which is going to be discussed later.

***Vyāpti* :**

**Formal definition of Vyāpti**

Like *parāmarśa vyāpti* or invariable concomitance essentially depends on two facts viz. the *vyāpya* (pervaded) and the *vyāpaka* (pervader). Thus, *vyāpti* is a correlation of these two facts. The pervaded one covers a narrow area whereas; pervader one covers a wider area. In simple language, the *vyāpaka* or pervader is present in all the places in which the *vyāpya* or the pervaded one is present. This theory generates a universal rule like 'where there is *vyāpya* there is *vyāpaka*'. The instance of smoke and fire can be considered here. Two notions can be drawn from the above instance like 'where there is smoke there is fire' and 'whatever possesses smoke possesses fire'. It suggests that smoke is pervaded by fire. In other words, fire is the pervader. But the reverse order is not true. In Prof. Wada's[19] language "The invariable concomitance of smoke with fire has been regarded as relation so far, but it can be considered to be the state of invariably co-existing with fire. The state of invariably co-existing with entity, smoke or fire, exists in smoke and not in fire. This is because fire does not possess the state of invariably co-existing with smoke, as in the case of the fire of a red-hot iron ball."

**Its role in the process of Inference**

Invariable concomitance plays a very important role in the process of inference. Without a universal relation between two facts (i.e. *vyāpya* and *vyāpaka)* no valid conclusion can be drawn from the premises[20]. Now, there is a disagreement between the logicians regarding the function of *vyāpti*. Some say that it functions as an instrument of the process of the inference[21] whereas, some hold it as a component involved in the process of inference. Again, *vyāpti* , based on unequal extention, such as smoke and fire, is called *viṣama-vyāpti* or *asama-vyāpti*. It is called so because there is a relation of non-equipollent between two terms like *vyāpya* and *vyāpaka,* from one of which we infer the other but not vice-versa[22]. For example, smoke and fire. But a *vyāpti,* which possesses equal extension between two terms, is called *samavyāpti* or equipollent concomitance. It happens to see between cause and effect, substance and attribute, etc. and also in vice-versa. For instance, 'whatever is produced is non-eternal' and 'whatever is non-eternal is produced'.

***Parāmarśa* :**

***Parāmarśa,* the knowledge of *Vyāptiviśiṣṭa-hetu* in the *pakṣa***

*Parāmarśa* or confirmatory cognition is produced with the help of two technical terms viz. *Vyāptiviśiṣṭa* and *pakṣadharmatājñāna*. Independently these two terms have their respective meanings but when they come altogether they generate a third kind of knowledge, which is nothing except *parāmarśa*. So, the nature of *parāmarśa* will be clarified when the nature of its components will be clearly understood. The compound *Vyāptiviśiṣṭapakṣadharmatājñāna* can be dissolved like *Vyāptiviśiṣṭa pakṣadharmatājñāna* (locative *tatpuruṣa)*. It means, 'that *pakṣadharmatājñāna* which is *Vyāptiviśiṣṭa* (the knowledge of the property of the subject which is qualified by invariable concomitance). Again, *Dīdhītikāra*[23] dissolves the compound like as *'Vyāptiviśiṣṭaṃ (vyāptiprakārakaṃ) yat pakṣadharmatājñānaṃ iti'*. In other words, *'yat pakṣadharmatājñānaṃ tat Vyāptiviśiṣṭaṃ'* (that the knowledge of the property of the subject is qualified by invariable concomitance). Here also the idea has been kept unchanged. *Nyāyabodhinī*[24] considers the compound as *karmadhāraya* keeping the meaning unchanged.

All the above definitions, given by various logicians, convey the same meaning. Hence, the conclusion can be drawn like *'vyāpti* is the *viśeṣaṇa* of the *hetu*'. Therefore, *parāmarśa* can be defined as 'the knowledge of *Vyāptiviśiṣṭa-hetu'* in the *pakṣa*.

In the of process inference, *parāmarśa* functions as an immediate cause. Of course, there is a controversy over this issue, which will be discussed later. According to *Naiyāyikas* this confirmatory knowledge functions as an immediate cause in the process of inference. This can be explained as follows:

**Function of parāmarśa**

A person, who has the experience of invariable concomitance of smoke and fire, sees a string of smoke on the mountain. And all of sudden he recalls the relationship which has been experienced in the kitchen etc. previously. Then he realizes like 'this (mountain) smoke is invariable associated with fire like kitchen'. This is called *parāmarśa* or confirmatory cognition. Immediately after that the inferential cognition like 'this mountain possesses fire' arises.

Finally, whether something is an instrument or function

of an instrument depends on the notion of an instrument *(karaṇa)*.

***Hetvābhāsa* :**

**It is not a real probans but appears to be so**

*Parāmarśa* generates inference and *hetu* is the ultimate cause of *parāmarśa*. A bad reason produces an invalid *parāmarśa* and invalid inference ultimately, which is not desired. Therefore, logicians have tried to find out the characteristics of a bad reason. This is, in logical terminology, is called *hetvābhāsa*. The compound *hetvābhāsa* has two terms, *hetu* and *ābhāsa*. *Hetu* in context of inference means 'ground or probans of inference' and *ābhāsa* literally means 'appearance or fault'. Thus, the term *hetvābhāsa* signifies either a 'seeming ground' or 'fault of a proposed ground'. These are the possible interpretations can be made out of the term *hetvābhāsa*. *Maharṣi Gotama*[25] has not mentioned any definition of *hetvābhāsa*. But it is *Vātsyāyana*[26] who has defined *hetvābhāsa* as 'those which arc not real probans because of not possessing the real characteristics of a probans, but which appears as a probans because of their similarities.

**Its varieties**

This definition of *hetvābhāsa* matches with the first definition given above. There is a difference of opinion regarding the types of *hetvābhāsa* among the old logicians. Gotama[27] mentions the number as five. *Vātsyāyana* also accepts it. But it is *Udyotakara,* who extends the meaning of the *sūtra* little further. *Vācaspati Miśra,* the commentator of *Nyāya-sūtra-bhāṣya-vārttika,* also agrees with him. On the other hand, neo-logicians also accept five types of *hetvābhāsas*. *Ācārya Gaṅgeśa,* the author of *tattvacintāmaṇi,* classified *hetvābhāsa* in to five and later logicians also have accepted it. Finally, five types of *hetvābhāsas* have been accepted in the system. Those are:

1) *Savyabhicāra hetvābhāsa:*
2) *Birudha hetvābhāsa:*
3) *Satpratipakṣa hetvābhāsa:*
4) *Asiddha hetvābhāsa:*
5) *Bādhita hetvābhāsa:*

**(1) Savyabhicāra hetvābhāsa:**

*Vyabhicara* means 'non-residing only in one place' or 'inconstancy' and *savyabhicāra* means 'that which exists with *vyabhicāra*'. The very nature of this fallacy or *hetvābhāsa* is it involves contradiction of probans with that of probandum. For example,

| | |
|---|---|
| proposition: | sound is eternal |
| reason: | because it is intangible |
| example: | whatever is intangible is eternal, as atoms |
| application: | so the sound (so the sound is intansible) |
| conclusion: | therefore, sound is eternal. |

Again

| | |
|---|---|
| proposition: | sound is non-internal |
| reason: | because it is intangible |
| example: | whatever is intangible, is non-eternal, as intellect |
| application: | so the sound (so the sound is intangible) |
| conclusion: | therefore, sound is non-eternal |

Here, intangibility is present in both the subject. There is no invariable concomitance between 'intangible' and 'eternal' or 'non-eternal'.

**It's division:**

**(a) *Sādharaṇa hetvābhāsa* : General definition**

It is called *sadhāraṇa* or common because it is found to be present in both the places[28] i.e. where the probandum is present and where the probandum is absent. For example, 'the mountain has fire, because it possesses smoke'. Here, fire is the faulty probans because it is found in both the cases i.e. where there is smoke, kitchen etc. and in the hot iron rod where smoke is not present.

### (b) *Asādhāraṇa hetvābhāsa* : Definition

The collocatedness of probans and probandum with certain rules and regulations formulates the knowledge of invariable concomitance. The very nature *as asādhāraṇa-hetvābhāsa* is it is neither present in similar instance *(sapakṣa)* nor in dissimilar instance *(vipakṣa)*. It resides only in the subject[29]. This is just opposite to the *Sādharaṇa hetvābhāsa*.

For example, 'sound is eternal, because it possesses the property called soundness'. The soundness is the reason here, which exists only in the similar instance *(sapakṣa)* but not in the contrary instances *(vipakṣa)*.

### (c) *Anupasaṃhārī hetvābhāsa:*

It is defined as the 'hetu' devoid of any supporting instances, both positive and negative, is called *anupasaṃhārī*.

'where there is '+x' there is '+y' (The positive instance) and

'where there is '-x' there is '-y' (the negative instance)

Here, subject includes all the objects of the reason and the relation of probans and probandum can not be found out either in positive instance or in negative instance. For example, 'all objects are non-eternal, because they are knowable'. Here, 'everything' is the subject. The *sādhya* is non-eternal and knowability is the reason.

Here, we cannot find any positive or negative invariable relation between probans and probandum, because the subject 'everything' exists in all the subjects. Nothing remains there outside of the subject to be taken as an example.

**(2) *Biruddha hetvābhāsa:***

The contradictory fallacy has been defined as 'the reason, which opposes what is to be established'. For example, 'sound is eternal, because it is produced'. Here, probans does not support to the probandum rather it goes against it.

In other words, it obstructs to the knowledge of correct inference.

**(3) *Satpratipakṣa hetvābhāsa:***

*'Sat'* means 'being presented (somewhere)' *and pratipakṣa* means 'counter thesis'. So, that which is present in both the thesises i.e. in the similar thesis as well as in the counter thesis is called *satpratipakṣa.* Let us have an example:
Similar thesis:

'The sprout etc. are produced by an conscious agent, because they are of the nature of effect, like flower etc.'
Counter thesis:

'The sprout etc. are not produced by an conscious agent, because they are not produced by any embodied being, like sky etc.'

In these examples, neither of two probans is capable of establishing the proposed probandum.

**(4) *Asiddha hetvābhāsa:***

The mark, which is being yet to be properly established is not different from the characteristics of the probandum. It occurs when the middle term is wrongly assumed in any of the premises and so cannot be taken to prove the conclusion.

For example, 'Shadow is a substance, because it is characterized by the movement.' This again is of three kinds such as:

**(a) *Āśayāsiddha hetvābhāsa:***

*Āśraya* means the resting place but in the context of inference it is the inferential subject *Āsrayāsiddha* means the subject is not known or non-existent.

**(b) *Svarupāsiddha hetvābhāsa:***

For example, 'Sky flower is fragrant'. Here sky flower (the subject) does not exist. *Svarūpa* means nature. The very nature of this *hetu* is that it is non-existent in the inferential subject. For example, 'sound is a quality, because it has visibility'. Sound possesses the property of hearing but not visibility. Therefore, visibility does not exist in the subject.

**(c) *Vyāpyatvāsiddha hetvābhāsa:***

The compound *Vyāpyatvāsiddha* means that in which '*vyāpyatva* is non-existent'. Again '*vyāpyatva*' means that which is qualified by *vyāpti* or invariable concomitance. In this case, there is no such type of relationship between the probans and the probandum. The peculiarity of this fallacy is that it requires a condition *(upādhi)*. That which is pervaded by the probandum but not the pervader of the probans is called a condition. For example, 'where there is contact of wet-fuel with fire there is smoke'. Here, the contact of wet fuel is a condition, which does not permit *vyāpti* to arise.

**(5) *Bādhita hetvābhāsa :***

'Fire is cold, because it is a substance'. Here, two *pramāṇas* are arising simultaneously i.e. perception and inference. And it is proved that perceptual cognition is stronger than inferential cognition because the later one is dependent on the former. Therefore, the inference becomes weak. So, the absence of the probandum is pervaded by another strong means of cognition is called contradicted fallacy.

## FOOTNOTES

1. Vide: TSA परामर्शजन्य ज्ञानमनुमितिः।
2. Vide: TSA व्याप्तिविशिष्टपक्षधर्मताज्ञानं परामर्शः।
3. Vide: TSA व्याप्यस्य पर्वतादिवृतित्वं पक्षधर्मता।
4. Vide: TSA साहचर्यनियमो व्याप्तिः।
5. पक्षो यः साधयितुमिष्ट इति–NBh. 1.1.33, TSA.
6. NS. and NBh. 1.1.41
7. NVTT. 1.1.41
8. TSA
9. सिषाधयिषाविरहविशिष्ट सिध्यभावः पक्षता। तद्वान् पक्ष–NSM।
10. TSA
11. NSM. Verse-70
12. व्याप्यस्य पर्वतादिवृत्तित्वं पक्षधर्मता, TSA
13. लिङ्गलिङ्गिनोः सम्बन्धद्वयो दर्शनेन लिङ्गस्मृतिरभिसम्बध्यते, NBh-1.1.5
14. उदाहरणसाधर्म्यात्साध्यसाधनं हेतु, N.S. 1.1.34
15. व्याप्तिवलेनार्थगमकं लिङ्गम्।–TB-2
16. TSA
17. ibid.
18. ibid.
19. ICNN, P-35
20. NTK, p-252
21. Mīmāṃsakas and Buddhists hold vyāpti as an instrument in the process of inference.
22. *Navya-Nayiyāyikas* say so.
23. Vide. NBn-2
24. ibid. as in *Nyāyakośa, p-* 475
25. Gotama mentions the name only in *Nyāya-sūtra*-1.1.1
26. लक्षणभावादहेतवो हेतुसामान्यात् हेतुवदाभासमानाः। NBh. 1.2.4
27. NS—1.2.4.
28. NSM, *anumānukhuṇda*
29. Ibid.

CHAPTER-III

# THEORY OF INFERENCE ACCORDING TO THE MĪMĀṀSAKAS

## General background

Every human behavior has two aspects such as: he thinks and he argues. He thinks because he observes. Again there are two means of human observation; he closely observes whatever he gets before him and he employs same knowledge, which is obtained from close observation, for the remote objects. So, direct perception and indirect perception are two means of knowing. Again, he argues because he tries to convince others about his own knowledge of truths. He tries to justify his own feelings in others. To do so, he develops a particular method or system of reasoning, which is otherwise called logic. To do so, he develops his ability to reason correctly. He seeks help of a systematic method of obtaining knowledge. This systematic method, through which he obtains a valid knowledge, is called *pramāṇa* and the science of its application is called *pramāṇaśāstra* or Epistemology.

The Indian philosophical systems have a serious dealing with this part. *Mīmāṁsā* system, in this connection, is in no way exceptional. The very existence of things, according to *Mīmāṁsakas,* is two fold such as: means of knowledge *(mana)* and objects of knowledge *(meya)*[1]. Here, this chapter deals with the means of knowledge according to *Mīmāṁsa system.* Before doing so let us discuss what knowledge is? And how it functions? The function of knowledge, according to *Mīmāṁsā* school of Indian philosophy, is to illuminate the things other than itself.[2]

Knowledge, as it is discussed in *Mīmāṁsā* system, is of two kinds valid and invalid. Valid knowledge is the knowledge of an unkown real knowledge[3]. The means of valid knowledge or *pramāṇas,* according to *Bhāṭṭa* school of *pūrva Mīmāṁsā,* is a knowledge which does not fail to recognize[4] whereas, Prabhākaras hold *pramāṇa* as 'valid knowledge' (but not the means of valid knowledge). He opines that *pramāṇa* or valid knowledge as 'experience, which is totally different from remembrance'[5]. However, the numbers of *pramāṇa,* according to *Kumārila Bhaṭṭa,* is six whereas, according to *Prabhākara* it is only five[6]. Those six *pramāṇas* are Perception, Inference, Similarity, Analogy, Presumption and Negation.

## Defination of *Anumāna*

Among these *pramāṇas,* inference or *anumāna* as defined in *Śābara Bhāṣya* is 'a cognition of an object not in direct contact and forming one of the two sides to a known relation, one of which is directly apprehended'[7]. Let us analyze the above definition of inference given by *Śabarasvāmīn*. This definition contains three necessary conditions. Those are *asannikṛṣṭe buddhiḥ, jñātasambadha* and *ekadeśadarśana.*

*Asannikṛṣṭe buddhiḥ* means, 'the knowledge of an object, which is not in direct contact with sense organs'. The term *'jñātasambadhasmaraṇa'* indicates that there should be a known relation between two objects, which are invariably related with each other.

*Ekadeśadarśana* means 'of which one should be directly apprehended'. It means out of those two objects, which are invariably connected with each other, one should be seen from a distance. In simple language, *ekadeśadarśana* refers to *vyāpya darśana*.

Now, let us organize this into a sequence.

| | | |
|---|---|---|
| First: | *ekadeśadarśana* | *(vyāpya darśana)* |
| Then: | *jñātasambadhasmaraṇa* | *(vyāpti smaraṇa)* |
| Finally: | *asannikruṣṭe buddhiḥ* | *(anumiti)* |

An example like 'this mountain possesses fire because of smoke' can present a clear picture of this format. According to *Mīmāṁsā* system, smoke is *ekadeśa (vyāpya)*, because it is pervaded by fire. The word *jñātasambadha* indicates to a known relation (say, relation of smoke and fire) i.e. 'where there is fire there is smoke'. So the process of inference in this system appears like this:

*Dhūma darśana*

*Vyāpti smaraṇa*

*Anumiti*

There is no scope for' application' on *parāmarśa* here as *Nyāya* holds. *Mīmāṁsakas* hold *'buddhi'* or knowledge as inference. From the above process of inference it is clear that *Mimāmsā* system does not require the third component called *parāmarśa* at all. There will be a discussion at length over this issue in seventh chapter.

This definition of inference as given by *Śabarasvāmīn,* contains two important terms like *jñātasambadha* and *asannikṛṣṭabuddhi*. These two terms have been interpreted by later *Mīmāṁsakas* in various ways. Let us discuss them one by one.

**Four alternative interpretations of jñātasambadha given by Kumārila : First interpretation**

*Kumārila Bhaṭṭa,* the author of *Ślokavārttika,* derives four possible alternative meanings of the term *jñātasambadha.* The first interpretation, as he suggests, is *pramātā jñāta-*

*sambadhaḥ*[8]. *Jñātasambadha* means the knower, who knows the invariable relationship of probans and probandum i.e. between smoke and fire. The compound has been dissolved by him in two ways such as: *bahuvrīhi* and *karmadhāraya*. When it is *bahuvrīhi it expresses the meaning like jñāta sambhadhaḥ yena saḥ*[9] (the knower, who already has experienced the *sambandha)*. When it is *karmadhāraya* it expresses the meaning like *jñātaḥ sambadhaḥ yatra*[10] (where the *sambadha* has been experienced i.e. *pakṣaekadeśa)*. Thus, the form of inference, according to his first interpretation, follows like this: when such a person *(pramātā,* who knows the invariable concomitance of smoke and fire) happens to see smoke from a distance (somewhere in the mountain), then he remembers the invariable concomitance and immediately the inferential concomitance i.e. this mountain possesses fire arises in him.

**Second interpretation:**

His second interpretation suggests that the compound may be explained as referring to the substratum *(ekadeśin)*, where the relationship of smoke and fire is apprehended[11]. Here, *jñātasambadha* stands for similar instances *(sapakṣa)*[12]. There are many places where smoke and fire are seen together like kitchen etc., And the most common place like mountain etc, where after observing smoke the fire is inferred. The former one is called *pakṣa* whereas the later one is called *sapakṣa*.

The *pakṣa* and *sapakṣa* both are *ekadeśin* (the instance) whereas smoke and fire both are *ekadeśa* (the relata). To fit the present context we may quote *Pārthasārathi Miśra's* definition of inference. Inference, according to him, is an *ekadeśa* (for example, smoke), of a *sapakṣaikadeśin* (for example, kitchen), where invariable concomitance of smoke and fire has already been recognized. And when it will be perceived in the *pakṣaeikadeśin* (i.e. mountain) there arises the cognition of another *ekadeśa* and this later cognition is called inference'[13]. Therefore, the form of inference on the basis of second interpretation is अनुमानं समक्षस्य एकदेशदर्शनादेक-देशान्तरे असन्निकृष्टे बुद्धिः।

**Third interpretation:**

The third alternative interpretation of *Kumārila Bhaṭṭa* takes a new turn. Here, he derives the meaning of the compound *jñātasambadha* as a 'known relationship'. He dissolves the term with the help of *karmdhāraya samāsa*[14]. And the word *ekadeśa* refers to a member of this relationship. The relationship only can occur between two terms and members, Here, the members are smoke and fire. So, the inference, according to his third interpretation, is the cognition of fire (say second member) of a known relationship holding from the perception of smoke i.e. first member.

**Fourth interpretation:**

The fourth possible interpretation of the compound *'jñātasambadha'* refers both *liṅga* and *liṅgin,* whose relationship is known[15]. That which includes another thing is called *liṅga* and *liṅgin* is that whose presence is inferred by *liṅga.* Smoke always indicates the presence of fire therefore it is *liṅga* and fire is being indicated by smoke therefore it is called *liṅgin.* Hence, inference occurs when on the perception of one part (smoke) of a logical whole, the cognition of the second part (fire) arises from a known relationship i.e. invariable concomitance between two parts[16].

***Prabhākara* theories of inference:**

On the other hand, *Prabhākara Mīmāṁsaka,* another commentator of *Sābara Bhāṣya,* interprets the compound *jñātasambadha* as a 'known relation'. So, the inference, in the words of *Prabhākara,* is 'a knowledge which arises of that which is not in contact with sense organs and which arises after the perception of one part[17]. Smoke is such an object whose relationship is established with fire and which takes place somewhere in the mountain. The knowledge of fire, which arises from the perception of the same, is not in contact with the sense organs.

**The interpretation of the word *asannikṛṣṭa* : Kumarila's interpretation:**

Further, both the *Mīmāṁsakas* have come forward to define the word *asannikṛṣṭa*. According to *Kumārilabhaṭṭa,* the word *asannikṛṣṭa,* which literally means 'not in contact with the sense organs', is non-determined. By giving the meaning 'non-determined' he means to exclude two things such as: 'the determination of the inferable object in that form' and 'the determination of that in the contrary form,'[18]. For example, the inferential cause like fire etc. According to him, if the very existence of inferable object i.e. fire will be previously determined through sense perception etc. then it would be a restatement here (i.e. in the case of inference). Similarly, it would be non-valid if it is determined as non-existing. Therefore, he has explained the term as non-determined.

***Prabhākara's* interpretation:**

On the other hand, *Prahhākar Mīmāṁsaka,* explains the term in a different way. According to him, the word *'sannikṛṣṭa'* means remembrance[19], and *asannikṛṣṭa* means that which is different from remembrance. Because this can be a cause to dust etc. As a matter of fact, *Śālikanātha,* the author of *Prakaraṇapañcikā,* explains the word keeping the meaning unchanged[20].

A comparative study of both the schools provides some notable observations. The way *Kumārila* explains is little complicated one. He gives all possible interpretations, from various angles. On the other hand, *Prahhākara's* definitions are seem to be simpler and to the point. Hence, the later one seems to be more approaching.

**Kinds of inference :**

**First type**

The tradition of classifying inference into *svārtha* and *parārtha,* perhaps, has been started from *Dignāga. Pre-Dignāga* school of Indian philosophy has nothing to say in this regard[21]. However, there is no reference of such division either in *Jaiminīya sūtra* or in *Śabara's* commentary. But in *Mānameyodaya* the inference has been divided into two such as: *svārtha* (inference for oneself) and *parārtha* (Inference for others).

***Svārthānumāna***

Inference for oneself *(svārtha)* occurs when fire etc. is inferred after seeing smoke etc. through the remembrance of invariable concomitance[22]. So, this process needs three steps.

| | |
|---|---|
| *Hetu darśana* | (perception of smoke somewhere in the mountain) |
| *Vyāptismaraṇa* | (remembrance of invariable concomitance of probans and probandum) |
| *Anumiti* | (the knowledge that there is fire on the mountain). |

A close observation can direct that the definition given by *Śabarasvāmīn* and that of present one is in no way different.

***Parārthānumāna***

The inference for others, as it is defined in *Mānameyodaya,* is 'some object (some inferable object i.e. fire etc.) are known through the words of another'. This is an inference of statements. Here, somebody after experiencing for himself tries to convince to somebody else through some statements.

Those statements, which are known as syllogism, are like this:

| | |
|---|---|
| Proposition *(pratijñā)* | 'mountain is fiery' |
| Reason *(hetu)* | 'because there is smoke' |
| Example *(udāharaṇa)* | 'where there is smoke there is fire as in the kitchen' |

Here, a further discussion continues regarding the numbers of *avayavas*. *Nārāyaṇa,* the author of *Mānameyodaya,* criticizes *Naiyāyikas* saying 'we, unable to put up with repetition, speak of three members, either ending with the example or beginning with the example'[23]. In either way they accept only three-membered syllogisms. We have seen the statement ending with example. Now let us see the proposition beginning with example.

| | |
|---|---|
| Example *(udāharaṇa):* | where there is smoke there is fire |
| Application *(upanaya):* | mountain possesses smoke (which is pervaded by fire) |
| Conclusion *(niganama):* | therefore, the mountain is fiery. |

*Mīmāṁsakas* hold that by premise the purpose of the conclusion and by the reason that all the application are served. Then why unnecessarily five statements will be accepted?

**Second type: *Pratyakṣhodṛṣṭa***

A further division of inference is available in the commentary of *Śabarasvāmīn* on *Jaiminīya Mīmāṁsā sūtra*[24]. He divides inference into two like *pratyakṣatodṛṣṭa sambdha* and *sāmānyatodṛṣṭa sambadha.* The definition of these terms has not been defined but has been illustrated by him. The commentator explains *pratyakṣatodṛṣṭa sambdha* as 'from the perception of smoke the form of fire is inferred'[25]. Because it is based on the relationship, that which is directly perceived. The relationship, which has been experienced previously somewhere in the kitchen etc. After remembering invariable relationship between smoke and fire, whenever, somebody sees smoke somewhere on the mountain, a certain knowledge arises in him like 'this mountain is fiery'. This is what is called *pratyakṣhodṛṣṭaṃ*.

### *Sāmānyatodṛṣṭa*

The inference that based upon a generalized relationship has been illustrated by *Śabara svāmīn* like this: one can infer that there is motion in the sun because it changes its place like other movable objeçts like *Devadatta* etc'[26]. Here, the movement of the sun cannot be perceived directly but can be inferred from its motion (i.e. changing place from time to time). So, from the above instance we can formulate a general statement like: 'whenever an object changes its place it has motion'. This instance is based upon a known fact. Therefore, it is called inference with generalized relationship or *sāmānyatodṛṣṭa sambadha*.

### Kumārila Bhaṭṭa's interpretation on second type : The above division carries no value

The above division of inference created a room for *Kumārila Bhaṭṭa* to raise an objection. He opposes it saying 'there is mutually exclusiveness between these two classes of inference'[27]. He finds no difference. The relation of smoke with fire is not directly seen. So all so the case of changing position and movement. On the other hand, if somebody claims saying that though the relationship is not directly seen but it has been experienced directly in kitchen etc. we reply them like the relation between change of position and movement is also cannot be seen directly but it can be assumed from the activities of *Devadatta*. Hence, both the illustrations can be applied in *sāmānyato-dṛṣṭa*[28].

He, therefore, rejects the term *pratyakṣatodṛṣṭa* and puts *viśeṣyatodṛṭa* in its place. According to *Kumārila,* a division must possess some unique characteristics. But it does not happen in case of *pratyakṣatodṛṣṭa* and *sāmānyatodṛṣṭa,* because *viśeṣa* is opposite to *sāmānya* but not to *pratyakṣa.*

### *Viśeṣyatodṛṣṭa*

*Viśeṣyatodṛṣṭa* or seen by particulars type of inference, according to *Kumārila Bhaṭṭa,* is based on an invariable relation between two particulars. It has been illustrated like this. A person observes a particular fire produced out of some fuel like cow dung etc. with its effect that is smoke. And one day he happens to see a particular string of smoke somewhere in the mountain then he remembers the relation between the two particulars and then he concludes that a particular fire exists on mountain, which is not in contact with our sense organs. It is called so because it is based upon a particular relation of a particular perception[29].

### Sāmānyatodṛṣṭa

On the other hand, *Sāmānyatodṛṣṭa* is knowledge of the relation by perception of two general objects. *Kumārila* keeps the idea unchanged with *Śabara* in this connection[30]. However, *sāmānyatodṛṣṭānumāna* deals with the class of objects. The example is the familiar inference of the fire with smoke in the hill.

### *Prahhakara Misra*'s interpretation on second type:

*Prahhākara Mīmāṁsakas* explain *Śabara's* division of inference in a different way. He classifies inference on the basis of the self-property of the object of inference *(sādhya).* Sometimes the self-property of the probandum is perceptible and sometimes it is imperceptible.

***Dṛṣṭasvalakṣaṇa* and *Adṛṣṭasvalakṣaṇa***

When it is perceptible it is called *dṛṣṭasvalakṣaṇa* and when it is not perceptible it is called *adṛṣṭasvalakṣaṇa*. So according to him, inference is of two kinds that is *dṛṣṭasvalakṣaṇa* and *adṛṣṭasvalakṣaṇa*[31]. The self-property of the object of inference that is fire-ness is perceptible. That is why this is the example of the first category[32]. But in the case of second one the self-property of the prabandum is imperceptible. For example, action or movement and potency *(śakti)*[33].

**Third type:**

Third type of classification of inference also has been accepted by the system. Of course, *Śabara Bhāśya* has nothing to say about it. *Prabhākaras* do not say anything about it also. *Kumārila Bhaṭṭa* also does not mention this classification. But it is *Nārāyaṇa*, the follower of *Bhaṭṭa* school of *Mimāṁsa*, who classifies inference into three like *anvaya-vyatireki*, *kevalānvayi* and *kevela-vyatireki*[34]. This classification is based upon the invariable concomitance.

***Kevalānvayi anumāna***

The first one is *kevalānvayi liṅga* or purely positively concomitant. The existence of Probandum where there is the existence of probans is called *kevalānvayi vyāpti* or positive pervasion. And inference, which possesses *anavayivyāpti* is called *kevalānvayi* or only positive inference[35]. For example, the knowledge manifested by another knowledge, because it's knowledge like jar etc. Here one cannot produce a negative example because all the objects can be illustrated by knowledge. As it is impossible to produce a negative example of the inference hence it is called *Kevalānvayi anumāna*.

***Kevala-vyatireki anumāna***

A *kevalavyatireki vyāpti* or only negative perversion

occurs there where the nonexistence of probans is seen in case of non-existence of the probandum.

And the inference, which possesses only negative invariable concomitance or *kevalavyatireki vyāpti,* is called only negative inference[36]. For example, every cognition is self-manifesting because it is cognition. Where there is no self-manifestedness there is absence of cognition-ness. For example, say a pot. Here it is not possible to produce a positive example i.e. what is self-manifesting is also a cognition. Therefore, it is calleci only negative inference.

***Anvayavyatireka anumāna***

That is called an inference of both positive and negative or *anvayavyatireka anumāna,* which contains both the type of invariable concomitance[37]. In other words, the inference containing both the positive and negative pervasion is called *anvayavyatireka.* For example, the mountain possesses fire because of smoke. We can have it in both the ways i.e. 'where there is smoke there is fire'—positive pervasion and 'where there is no smoke there is no fire'—negative pervasion. And the combination of both the pervasions generates a third one called positive and negative pervasion as well.

Among these three types of inferences, the followers of Kumarila, however, do not accept the only negative inference[38]. And in its place they put the fifth variety of valid knowledge called *anupalabdhi.*

**The constituents of inference : Nature and function of the components**

The key component of the process of inference is *vyāpti* because it brings together two things i.e. *vyāpya* and *vyāpyaka* in a certain rule. Again, *vyāpya* and *vyāpaka* exist on a locus called *pakṣa.* The validity of inference is totally dependent on a good *hetu.* Therefore, in this context, *hetvābhāsa* will be discussed. So, we have components called *pakṣa, sādhya, hetu, vyāpti* and *hetvābhāsa.* On the other hand, *'avayavas'* which are engaged by the system to generate inference in others; are also supposed to be discussed here. Now let us define these components first as it is discussed in *Mīmāṁsā* system.

**Pakṣa**

*Pakṣa,* otherwise called *ekadeśin,* has been defined by *Mīmāṁsakas* as 'that which is qualified by the property (namely *sādhya),* whose very existence is doubtfull'[39]. It is called *ekadeśin* because it possesses a property called *'ekadeśi'* (' *ekadeśaḥ-asti iti ekadeśin').* This is a substratum or locus of both *vyāpya* and *vyāpaka. Vyāpya,* which is already known, and *vyāpaka,* which is to be known through *vyāpya.* When such situation will arise there that will be considered as *pakṣ a.* But when the attribute (say, fire) does not make one to be desired to know then what is qualified by such attribute will not be considered as *pakṣa*[40]. In their terminology it is called *pakṣābhāsa* or a fallacious subject (which is going to be discussed later).

**Hetu:**

*Mīmāṃsakas* define *hetu* or probans as 'that which is pervaded and having either instrumental attribute.'[41] So, which is pervaded by the probandum and having an instrumental attribute is called a probans or reason.

**The definition of *hetu***

It is also called *'gamaka'* because it leads to knowledge of something, which is not directly seen. It is a sign or indicator of the thing that which is going to be inferred. Hence, it is called *liṅga.* It is called, on the other hand, a *hetu* because this is the only cause of the establishment of the probandum. Because it is the only means of proving the probandum so it is called as *sādhana.* It has another epithet called *niyamya* also. In *Mīmāṁsā* system the invariable association of *vyāpya* and *vyāpaka* is called *niyama*. In this case, *vyāpya* (say, smoke) is *niyamya* and *vyāpaka* (say, fire) is *'niyāmaka* '. The former is being controlled by the later[42]. However, on the basis of reason or *hetu* the invariable object is supposed to be established.

**Its variety:**

*Mīmāṁsakas* also have classified reason into three varieties like: *anvaya-vyatireka liṅga* or positive negative mark, *kevalānvayi liṅga* or only positive mark and *kevalavyatireki liṅga* or only negative mark[43]. Let us discuss the nature and function of these marks.

***Anvaya-vyatireka liṅga*:**

*Mīmāṁsakas,* in this regard, are in no way different from that of *Naiyāyikas*. The reason or mark, which possesses both the type of invariable concomitance, is called *anvyaya-vyatireki-liṅga*. This reason or mark has named after *'anvyaya-vyatireka-vyāpti'* because the nature of *hetu* is dependent on *vyāpti*. Here, *anvyaya-vyāpti* or positive invariable concomitance is the invariable concomitance between probans and probandum. In other words, where there is presence of probans there is presence of probandum. Again, *vyatireka-vyāpti* or negative invariable concomitance occurs between the absence of probans and the absence of probandum. We have an example like 'mountain possesses fire, because of smoke'. Here, smoke has both the invariable concomitances i.e. positive and negative. Therefore, it is called positive and negative mark.

***Kevalānvayi liṅga:***

The mark, which possesses the symptoms of a positive invariable concomitance, is called a positive invariable concomitance mark. Here, the opposite site of positive invariable concomitance cannot be observed. For example, 'the pot is namable because it is knowable, like cloth etc.' The only positive invariable concomitance like 'where there is knowability there is namebility'[44] can be produced out of this example. But the other part cannot be experienced. Hence, it is called only negative mark.

***Kevalavyatireki liṅga:***

The mark or *liṅga* possessing only negative invariable concomitance is called only negative mark. Here, we can't produce any positive invariable concomitance. For example, 'the Earth is different from other substances, because it has smell'. Its opposite example cannot be experienced. Here, smoke possessing only negative invariable concomitance; hence it is named after it.

**Characteristics of a *sad-hetu* :**

It has been mentioned that the validity of inference is totally dependent on the validity of the reason. In other words, a good reason or *sad-hetu* has the potentiality to produce a valid inference. Therefore, logicians are very conscious to determine whether the *hetu* is true or fallacious, *Mīmāṁsakas* have determined characteristics of a good reason as well as that of a bad one.

It is mentioned in *Mānameyodaya*[45] that the positive and negative concomitance has five aspects such as: being the attribute of the subject *(pakṣadharmatva)*, existence in the co-subject *(sapakṣesattvaṃ)*, non-existence in the counter-subject *(vipakṣadvayāvṛttitvaṃ)*, un-contradictory *(abādhittvaṃ)* and having no counter probans *(asatpratipakṣattvaṃ)*.

The first one suggests that the reason should be present on the inferential ground only. For example, the hill is fiery. because of smoke'. Here, the reason i.e. smoke has to be present otherwise a valid inference cannot be drawn at all.

The second aspect of a good reason is that it is supposed to be present only in co-subject or similar instances[46]. For example, kitchen etc., where the smoke exists along with fire.

The third aspect of a good reason is its absence in counter subject[47]. For example, a big lake etc., where the non-existence of probandum is not known. That is to say that in a lake etc. we cannot find the presence of probandum and probans as well.

Its fourth aspect is that it must be un-contradicted by some other strong proofs. For example, if it is said that fire is cold, because it is a substance', then there will be a contradiction. Because, the coldness of fire is not experienced. Hence, there should not arise any contradiction.

Non-existence of an opposite probandum is having no counter probans. In other words, there should not be two equal strong reason i.e. the absence of probandum, which is related to the reason should not be contradicted. called a positive invariable concomitance mark.

However, a mark or reason possessing both the concomitance i.e. positive and negative, has the above five aspects. The only positive mark has only four aspects, because it has non-existence in the counter subject. The only negative mark has also four aspects, because it has non-existence in the similar instance. Therefore, only positive and negative mark can satisfy all above mentioned five conditions.

Characteristics of a bad reason have been discussed in later part of this chapter.

**Vyāpti:**

The term *vyāpti* is not found either in *Mīmāṁsā sūtra* or in *Śābara bhāṣa*. He only mentions the term *'sambandha'* in the commentary, which, in later period, has been explained by the sub-commentator as *vyāpti*[48].

**_Vyāpti_ in the language of _Kumārila Bhaṭṭa_**

*Kumārila Bhaṭṭa* says '*sambandha*' is nothing but an invariable concomitance between *liṅga* and *liṅgin*. *Liṅga* or *vyāpya* is one which appears either in all cases of the *vyāpaka* or in some cases, but *vyāpaka* or *liṅga* exists in all cases of *vyāpya*[49]. In other words, where there is probans there is probandum but not the vice-versa. However, he holds invariable concomitance as a necessary condition of the process[50]. According to him, the means of invariable concomitance is the experience of co-instances in different times and places[51]. It is the repeated observation of the existence of smoke where there is fire, which formulated a universal relation. This relation is nothing but *vyāpti*. He further tells that *vyāpti* is a necessary condition generally between two universals, but sometimes it is a relation of two particulars. The example for the first case is smoke and fire, whereas, *Kṛttikā* and *Rohiṇi* is the example of the second case.

**Prabhakara's interpretation**

Now what *Prabhākara* school of *Pūrva Mīmāṁsā* holds is that a single observation *(sakṛtdarśana)* is enough for the knowledge of *vyāpti*. He entertains a condition *(upādhi)* saying 'repeated observation *(bhūyodarśana'* or togetherness of *hetu* and *sādhya* is useful in showing it i.e. *upādhi*. *Prabhākara* holds *vyāpti* as a *niyama,* which is a natural relation. *"Niyana",* says Govinda P. Bhatta, "is the empirical law of invariable association of two things on the basis of which the knowledge of one of the things leads to the knowledge of another. This empirical law may imply any kind of relation between two things and the inference based on it is strictly in accordance with the past of the relation"[52]. However, this natural relation means the relation without any condition *(upādhi)*. Condition or *upādhi* is that which is said to be another reason to lead probandum directly[53]. In short, the relation between fire and smoke is a conditional *(aupādhika),* whereas, the relation between smoke and fire is natural *(anaupādhika)*. The former one needs another factor (say, wet fuel), which is the pervader of the probandum. But the later one does not require such things. An example can make clear this point. One can state that 'there is smoke because there is wet fuel connection. But one need not say that 'where there is wet fuel contact there is fire'. The first one is the example of conditional relation whereas the second one is that of natural.

**Conditions of a valid inference:**

Inference for others' sake, as it occurs in *Mīmāṁsā* system, is greatly dependent on three constituent propositions such as: *pratijñā*, *hetu* and *udāharaṇa*. The validity of inference depends on these three factors. If either of these is proved to be fallacious then the whole inference will be proved as invalid. Therefore, like Buddhist logicians[54], *Mīmāṁsakas,* more particularly *Kumārila Bhaṭṭa,* has indicated the fallacious grounds corresponding three factors such as: *pratijñābhāsa, hetvābhāsa and dṛṣṭāntābhāsa*[55]. Theses are the key components of the process that's why it is necessary to determinate their fallacious aspects.

***Pratijñābhāsa* : The definition**

*Sucarita Miṣra,* while commentating *Ślokavārttika,* defines *pratijñibhāsa* as *sādhyanirdeśa*[56]. Proposition or *pratijñā* is a statement of establishing the object of inference *(sādhya)*. *Sādhaya* should not be previously known (ताद्रूप्येण गृहीतत्वं) and it should not be in a contradicted form (तद्विपर्य-यतोऽपि). If it is previously known then there is no need of re-establishing it. And if it is contradicted by another means of valid knowledge then it cannot be established. In other words, an unknown and un-contradicted statement is called a proposition. If it is proved to be otherwise then it will be known as *pratijñābhāsa* or the fallacies of inferential subject.

*Nārāyaṇa,* classifies fallacious proposition into three such as: (1) *siddhaviśeṣaṇa,* (2) *bādhitaviśeṣaṇa* and (3) *aprā-siddhaviśeṣaṇa*[57]. Let us discuss them briefly.

**The division**

If a proposition is already known by perception and still it is going to be inferred then it will be called as *siddhaviśeṣaṇa pratijñābhāsa.* For example, "fire is hot".

The second one occurs when a proposition is contradicted by another stronger *pramāṇa* then it is called as *badhitaviśeṣ aṇa pratijñābhāsa.* For example, "fire is not hot". The third one is *aprasiddhaviśeṣaṇa pratijñabhāsa,* which is not an established fact. From example, "Earth etc. has an omniscient creator". Here, it is not a known fact, because we don't find such things in a jar etc.

***Hetvābhāsa* : Classification of *hetvābhāsas***

There is no reference of *hetvābhāsa* or fallacies of inferential subject either in *Jaiminīya sūtra* or in *Śabara bhāṣya.* The later commentators like *Kumārila Bhaṭṭa.* and *Prabhākara Miśra* have determined it. Of course, different opinions can be notified between these two over this issue. *Kumārila's* classification seems to be little controversial[58]. But *Mānameyodaya,* a treatise of *Bhaṭṭa* school, presents a clear picture of this class of fallacies. On the other hand, *Pārthasārathī Miśra* also brings into notice of an improved classification of fallacies of probans in his treatise called *Śātradīpikā*[59].

*Hetvābhāsa,* according to *Mīmāṁsā* system, generally is of three kinds viz. *asiddha, aneikāntika* and *bādhita*[60]. Of course, there is a controversy regarding on it like when Pundit *Narāyaṇa* adds one more (i.e. *asādhāraṇa hetvābhāsa)* to the list then *Kumārila* considers it as a subdivision[61].

***Asiddha hetvābhāsa* : असिद्धहेतुदोषः**

*Asiddha* or un-established reason is the absence of the knowledge of the probans, which is qualified by invariable concomitance, is related to the subject[62]. It is of five kinds such as: *svarūpāsiddha, sambandhāsiddha, vyatirekāsiddha, āśrayāsiddha, vyāpyatvāsiddha*[63]. In the case of *svarūpāsiddha,* the very nature of the reason is un-established. For example, "Buddha is the knower of both *dharma* and *adharma*". Here, the reason omniscience is an imaginary character. Hence a valid conclusion cannot be drawn. *Sambandhāsiddha* denies the relation. For example, "the fire does not burn, because it is cold". Hence, it is not a valid knowledge. Where the identity of both *pakṣa* and *hetu* becomes one and same the *vyatirekāsiddha* fallacy arises there. For example, "Cow is an animal having dewlap etc., because it is denoted by the word 'cow'. Here, the inferential subject and the reason are one and same. *Āśrayāsiddha* mainly denies the *āsraya* or substratum of the reason. For example, "the sky lotus is fragrant, because it is a flower". In the case of *vyāpyatvā-siddha* the reason resides only in a part of the inferential subject. For example, "air and space are non-eternal, because they are tangible."

**अनैकान्तिकहेतुदोषः**

When the reason exists in both the subjects (i.e. inferential subject and its counter subject) then that will be called as non-conclusive fallacy[64]. It is again of two kinds like: *savyabhicāra* and *sapratisādhana*[65]. *Kumārila* adds the third variety introducing the term called *asādhāraṇa*[66]. When a fallacy entertains a contradiction of probans with probandum then that will be called as *savyabhicārin hetvābhāsa.* For example, "sound is eternal, because it is intangible". Here, intangibility (probans) does not regularly accompany eternity (probandum). *Sapratisādhan hetvābhāsa* occurs there where two contradictory reason emphasize the same object (i.e. object of inference) are both are equally strong. For example, "air is perceptible, because it is a substance and it is formless". Again "air is imperceptible, because it is a substance without color". Here, both the arguments are equally strong.

**बाधितहेतुदोष:**

The very nature of this fallacy is that it contradicts and does not allow probandum to be proved. It proves the absence of the probandum instead of proving its existence. For example, "sound is eternal, because it is produced". This is also called *Bādita* or obstructer because it does not allow inference to be proved as a valid inference.

### *Dṛṣṭāntābhāsa* : Its division and classification

*Dṛṣṭāntābhāsa* means fallacious example. And an example, in definition of the author of *Mānameyodaya,* is a place where the pervasion of probans and Probandum is established. This is the place where the object of the inference and its cause are present with a certain rule. This is again of two kinds such as: *sādharmya* (positively similar) and *vaidharmya* (negatively similar). "What has smoke has fire, like a kitchen etc.," is the example of the former one and "what has not fire does not have smoke, like water." If, in any case, the example happens to be fallacies then the whole inference will be invalid. Therefore, it is necessary to know the nature and function of the fallacious examples. However, *Nārāyaṇa* has classified the similar instance into four like: devoid of the object of the instance *(sādhyahīna),* devoid of probans *(sādhanahīna),* devoid of both i.e. prouans and probandum *(ubhayāhīna)* and devoid of substratum *(Āśraya-hīna).* Similarly, dissimilar example also has been divided into four kinds such as: *sādhyāvyāvṛtta* (not absent from the probandum), *sādhanāvyavṛtta* (not absent from the probans), *ubhayāvyāvṛtta* (not absent from both) and *Aśrayahīna* (devoid of base)[67].

However, the entire discussion of *Nārāyaṇa* is based upon *Ślokavārtika*[68].

**Observation : Similarities and dissimilarities**

A comparative study of the process of inference of both the systems provides some notable observations. Though *Mīmāṁsā* system has a different interpretation of inference still the process remains unchanged. The invariable association of *vyāpya* and *vyāpaka* is called *niyama. Nayiyāyikas* accept five membered syllogisms whereas, *Mīmāṁsakas* reduce it into three. *Nyāya* system accepts five *hetvābhāsas* whereas *Mīmāṁsa* accepts only three. In some points they are in one track. For example, *āśrayāsiddha hetvābhāsa, savyabhicāra hetvābhāsa* etc., whereas in some points they in a different track. For example, regarding *avayavas,* numbers of *hetvābhāsas* etc. However, in spite of lots of similarities and dissimilarities both the systems have accepted inference as a means of valid knowledge.

## FOOTNOTES

1. MM-1 मानमेयविभागेन वस्तुना द्विविधा स्थितिः।
2. SV-44 प्रतीतिः वस्त्वन्तरप्रकाशस्वभावा।
3. MM-verse no. 1
4. NR on SV, verse. 44 अविसंवादि विज्ञानं प्रमाणम्।
5. PP, p. 42 प्रमाणमनुभूतिः।
6. MM - verse no. 15
7. SBh. 1.1.5 अनुमानं ज्ञातसम्बन्धस्यैकदेशदर्शनादेकदेशान्तरेऽसन्नकृष्टे बुद्धिः।
8. SV-2, verse-3
9. Ibid, verse 3-4
10. This is also *Bahubrīhi*
11. Ibid.... एकदेश्यथवोच्यते।
12. NR, p.291 यस्य ज्ञातसम्बन्धस्य महानसाख्यो सपक्षो ज्ञातः।

13. Ibid.
14. *SV-2, verse* 3, कर्मधारयपक्षो वा सम्बन्धिन्येकदेशता।
15. NR, p. 291 लिङ्ग लिङ्गि द्वयं तत्समुदाय एव ज्ञातसम्बन्धः।
16. SV-2, verse 3, द्वये वा ज्ञातसम्बन्धमुपलब्धं परस्परम्।
तस्यैकदेशशब्दाभ्यमुच्यते समवायिनौ।।
17. *Bṛhati,* 1.1.5 अनुमानमेकदेशदर्शनादेकदेशान्तरे असन्निकृष्टेर्थे बुद्धिः। कस्यैकदेशस्य? ज्ञातसम्बन्धस्य।
18. SV-2 verse 55 असन्निकृष्टवाचा च द्वयमत्र जिहासितम्।
ताद्रूप्येण गृहितत्वं तद्विपर्ययतोऽपि च।।
19. *Bṛhati,* 1.1.5, सन्निकृष्टावमर्शे हि स्मरणमेव मन्यन्ते।
20. असन्निकृष्टपदं स्मरणाभिमाननिरासार्थमित्युक्तम्। –विषमस्थलाटिप्पणी on PP, अनुमानपरिच्छेद, p.196
21. EBPM, p. 254
22. MM, p. 63
23. MM, p. 63
24. SBh, 1.1.5
25. Ibid.
26. Ibid.
27. SV, verse 138
28. Ibid, verse 140
29. Ibid, verse 140-142
30. Ibid, verse 145
31. PP, p. 214 प्रमेयमनुमानस्य दृष्टादृष्टस्वलक्षणम्।
32. Ibid.
33. Ibid.
34. MM, p. 53 तच्चानुमानं त्रिविधं अन्वयव्यतिरेकि केवलान्वयि केवलव्यतिरेकि चेति।
35. MM, p. 53 साधनस्य सद्भावे साध्यस्यपि सद्भावः अन्वयव्याप्तिः।
36. Ibid. साध्यस्याभावे साधनस्याप्यभावः व्यतिरेकव्याप्तिः।
37. Ibid. तत्र यस्योभयविधाव्याप्तिरस्ति तदन्वयव्यतिरेकि।
38. Ibid, p. 56 ते च कौमारिलाः प्रायो नेच्छन्ति व्यतिरेकिणम्।
39. MM, p. 66 जिज्ञासितधर्मविशिष्टस्य पक्ष इत्युक्तम्।
40. Ibid. व्याप्यः साधनधर्मो हेतुः।
41. MM, p. 59
42. EBPM, p. 214
43. MM, *anumānaparichheda*

44. Ibid.
45. Ibid.
46. Ibid.
47. Ibid.
48. SV, verse 31/2, सम्बन्धोव्याप्तिरिष्टात्र लिङ्गधर्मस्य लिङ्गिना।
49. Ibid, verse 6, येन व्याप्यगृहितेऽर्थे व्यापकस्तत्र गृह्यते।
50. Ibid.
51. Ibid.
52. EPSB, p. 227
53. MM, p. 26, उपाधिरिति च साध्यस्य साक्षात्प्रयोजक हेत्वन्तरमुच्यते।
54. See first chapter
55. MM, p. 59, अथप्रतिज्ञाहेत्वोश्च दृष्टान्तस्य च दूषणम्।
    क्रमेण कथ्यतेऽस्याभिरर्थद्भेद्यं वादिनं पुरः।।
56. Comm. on verse no-54,
57. MM, p. 66 असिद्धोविरुद्धोऽनैकान्तिकोऽसाधारणश्चेति चत्वारस्तदाभासाः।
58. EBPM, p. 273
59. *Śāstradīpikā hetvābhāsa prakaraṇa.*
60. SD, p. 120 असिद्धः अनैकान्तिकत्वम् वाधितत्वम् चेति त्रयो हेतुदोषाः।
61. It will be discussed later.
62. SD, p. 120
63. Ibid.
64. Ibid.
65. Ibid, p. 121
66. EBPM, p. 275
67. MM, p. 89
68. SV, verse 108-137

CHAPTER - IV

# THEORY OF INFERENCE ACCORDING TO PRĀCĪNA NYĀYA

## General background

Philosophy deals with concepts. Concepts like soul, liberation etc. It characterizes the concepts and finally establishes it on the basis of a set of reasoning. The application of this set of reasoning gives birth to various intellectual traditions, which are otherwise called *hetuvidyā* or *hetuśāstra*. This *hetuśāstra* changed into *tarkaśāstra* later on when the reasons were indebted by a group of intellectuals. This fact briefs the history of origin and development of Indian philosophical traditions. Now let us turn our look into the internal affair of the systems. Systems are divided into subsystems, because of the method of application of its logicians, because of the method of clarification *(pariṣkāra-paddhati)*. Another possible cause of its division could be the debate among themselves. They examine the statement and take forward to discourse. This helped in the emergence of the system called *"Navya-Nyāya"*. However, this chapter deals with origin and development of inference starting from *Gotama* to *Udayana* (i.e. from 200 B.C. to 1050-1100 A.D.).

## Theory of inference according to Gotama:

*Nyāyasūtra* is the first systematic writing of this tradition.

The authorship of this magnum opus is attributed to *Gotama*[1], who seems to have flourished around 200 B.C. *Nyāyasūtra* mainly deals with the nature of objects *(prameya)*. Therefore, it is called the science of objects or *prameyaśāstra*. However, the author has given a primary importance to the instruments of obtaining valid knowledge *(pramāṇa)* by placing it at the very outset of the book[2].

### *Pramāṇa in Prācīna Nyāya*

According to him, the correct judgement of the nature of the sixteen categories (among *which pramāṇa* has been placed first) leads to salvation. It seems that *pramāṇa* is a member of the class of sixteen categories formulated by *Gotama* for application of *anumāna*. He does not give any definition of *pramāṇa* anywhere but he classifies it into four viz. *pratyakṣa* (perception), *anumāna* (inference), *upamāna* (comparison) and *śabda* (verbal understanding)[3].

### The theory so far

After defining *pratyakṣa Gotama* proceeds to explain *anumāna*. He defines *anumāna* as "preceded by it"[4]. It is understood that it refers to *pratyakṣa* (which has been pointed out by the commentators later), which has been discussed in the previous *śutra*. So, he means to say that inference is greatly dependent on perception. In simple language, inference requires a previous perceptual knowledge like if a river is banked then it can be inferred that there was a rainfall etc. Now opponents raise an objection saying, "inference cannot be a means of valid knowledge, because it suffers from *vyabhicāra*" (he raises this question in the *sūtra* no 2.1.37). He immediately replies saying that our inference based on something else other than the part, fear etc[5]. In this way, he has established the authority of inference but has not mentioned a systematic process of it. He only mentions name of the members of syllogism *(avayavas),* the name of components like *hetu, sādhya, hetvābhāsa* etc., in the *sūtra*. It implies that he is referring to *parārthānumāna*. There is no reference about *vyāpti* as well. However, later logicians have arranged these components into a sequence.

*Gotama* divides inference into three types such as: *pūrvavat, śeṣavat* and *sāmanyatodṛṣṭa*[6], but he does not give any definition of these divisions. However, these terms have been explained by later commentators.

**Members of syllogism**

*Sūtrakāra* mentions nothing about *parārthtānumāna,* but defines the members of syllogism. These are of five types such as: *pratijñā, hetu*, *udāharaṇa, uapanaya* and *nigamana*[7]. A proposition or *pratijñā* is the declaration of what is going to be established *(sadhyanirdeśaḥ)*. This is a statement, which is supposed to be ascertained with the help of other members of syllogism. *Hetu* is an establishing factor. He defines *hetu* or reason as the means for establishing the object of inference *(sāḍhya)* through the homogeneous *(sādharmya)* and heterogeneous *(vaidharmya)* character of the example[8]. He also uses synonyms like *liṅga, sādhana* etc. *Udāharaṇa* or example is of two kinds such as: *sādharmya* or homogeneous and *vaidharmya* or heterogeneous[9]. A *sadharmya udāharaṇa* possesses the thing that which is going to be established *(sādhyasādharmyāt)* and that which implies its opposite i.e. which does not possess the object of inference is called *vaidharmya udāharaṇa*. *Upạnaya* or application, as he defines, is dependent upon example *(udāharaṇasāpekṣa)*. Though he has not mentioned any division of *upanaya* still its two division is understood because of its dependency on the *udāharaṇa*. The *sādhrmya upanaya* can be concluded with the statement like "it is so" *(tathā)* and the *vaidharmya upanaya* can be concluded with the statement like "not like so" *(na tathā)*[10]. *Nigamana* is the affirmation of the proposition *(pratijñāyāḥ punarvacanaṃ)*[11]. It is the confirmation of the proposed statement after the reason *(hetvāpadeśāt)*.

Except these, the term like *sādhya* also occurs for several times in the *sūtra* but there is no definition of it. Similarly, the concept of *vyāpti* is also not found in the Gotama *sūtra*. Though he mentions the term like *pakṣa* but not in sense of 'inferential ground' but in the sense of 'side' (i.e. *svapakṣa, parapakṣa* etc.).

**Hetvābhāsa**

According to *Maharśi Gotama,* the proper knowledge of *hetvābhāsa* is one of the means of attaining the ultimate peace[12]. He does not define it but classifies it into five such as *savyabhicāra, viruddha, prakaraṇasama, sādhyasama and kālātita*[13]. *Savyabhicāra hetvābhāsa* is *aneikāntika*. It means not one pointed i.e. the reason, which leads to more than one conclusion[14]. He further defines *viruddha hetvābhāsa* or contradictory fallacy as reason, which opposes what is supposed to be established[15]. A reason is supposed to be an indicator of the object of inference but in spite of being so it contradicts it. Hence it is called a contradictory fallacy. *Prakaraṇasama hetvābhāsa* is such a fallacious reason, which intends to establish something but produces doubt regarding the same *(prakaraṇa cintā)*[16]. The fallacious reason that which is not different from *sādhya (sādhya aviśiṣṭa)* because it requires to be established *(sādhyatvāt)* is called *sādhyasama hetvābhāsa*. A proposition always stands to be proved but in this case the reason itself needs another proof to be proved[17]. And *Kālātita* or mistimed is a fallacious reason which is assigned after lapse of time *(kālātyayāpadiṣṭa)*[18]. However, the later logicians of this school will discuss these fallacious reasons elaborately with their respective examples.

This much information we get from *Gotama* on the theory of inference. Though examples are not provided still he provides the basic framework of inference, which grows and bears fruit in the later period after a due care of a number of logicians in the form of gardeners.

**Theory of inference according to *Vātsyāyana:***

*Vātsyāyana* is supposed to be the earliest commentator of *Nyāya-sūtra* of Gotama. Though, a controversy has been entertained by various scholars like 'he is not the first commentator of *Nyāya-sūtra*'[19] still they are in agreement that the earliest work on *Nyāya-sūtra* available to us is the commentary of *Vātsyāyana*. He is also known as *Pakṣila-swāmi, Drāmila*[20]. However, his time, as has been fixed approximately, is 450 A.D.[21].

*Pramāṇa,* according to *Vātsyāyana,* is *arthavat* (i.e. invariably connected with the object) because successful activity *(samartha-pravṛtti)* results when the object *(artha)* is verified by *pramāṇa*[22]. He holds *pramāṇa* as instrument of valid knowledge. However inference, as he defines, is 'the after knowledge *(paścāt māna)* of an object *(artha)* through a reason *(Liṅga),* which is rightly ascertained *(mita)*[23]. That is to say that probans and probandum are invariably connected. *Vātsyāyana* further defines inference while he comments *Nyāyasūtra* 1.1.5. Here, he gives clarification of the word *"tatpūrvaka"*. By the expression The *'tatpūrvaka'* (preceded by it) he means 'the perception of the inferential theory relation between the probans and the probandum' as well as 'the perception of the probans'[24]. Hence perception, according to *Vātsyāyana,* is twofold. Firstly the perception of invariable relationship of probans and the probandum and secondly perception of the probans. Again, the perception of relation (i.e. invariable relation of probans and probandum) causes the confirmation of the probans. And that 'perception' results into the inference of the object, which is not directly cognized[25].

So, the process of inference) as *Vātsyāyana* depicts, follows like this:

| | |
|---|---|
| 1. *liṅgaliṅgino sambandhadarśana* | perception of invariable relation of *liṅga* and *liṅgi* |
| 2. *sambandha smṛti* | recollection of the relation of probans and probandum. |
| 3. *apratyakṣya-artha-anumāna* | inference of the object of indirect perception. |

Thus, inference depends on these three steps. Here, he has not mentioned anything about *parāmarśa*.

**Two alternative definitions of the division:**

*Vātsyāyana* offers two alternative explanations of the division of inference. His first alternative explanation of the division is based on cause and effect relationship whereas the second type is based on the different method of establishing *vyapti*[26] (as later logicians have defined it).

**First explanation**

The inference of effect from its cause is called *pūrvavat*[27]. This effect should be immediately prior to it (i.e. cause). For example, the inference of a future rainfall from a heavy dark cloud. *Śeṣavat* inference is the inference of a cause from its effect[28]. For example, from the fullness and swift current of the river, we infer that there was a rainfall on the mountain. The former one is called *kāraṇaliṅgaka* because from the cause only the effect is being inferred whereas the later one is called *kārya-liṅgaka* because from the effect the cause is going to be inferred. *Samānyatodṛṣṭa,* as its name suggests, is a notion of generality. Of course, there is no definition of

*Sāmānyatodṛṣṭānumāna* in *Nyāyabhāṣya,* but its example characterizes it as an inference of general co-relation. For example, the perception of an object at some places which was previously somewhere else[29]. Because of its movement it changed the place. It means, we can draw an invariable relation like whatever changes its place is preceded by movement. Such general perception of invariable relation leads one to infer that the sun has movement because it changes its place.

**Second alternative explanation**

Perhaps *Vātsyāyana* was not satisfied with the first explanation so he stated explaining it further saying *"athavā purvavaditi"*[30]. Or it could be the case that he has quoted some other commentator's view (as he is not supposed to be the immediate commentator of *Nyāyasūtra)*[31]. However, *Vātsyāyana* has given second alternative explanation of the division of inference. *Pūrvavat,* as he defines alternatively, is the inference when an object, which is not in direct contact with the sense organs *(apratyakṣya),* is inferred through the perception of two objects *(yathāpūrvapratyakṣobhūta-anyataradarśan)* as they were previously perceived[32]. For example, perception of smoke etc. somewhere in the mountain helps to infer fire, which is not in direct contact. The word *Śeṣavat* means residual *(pariśeṣa)*. Hence, the inference of residual is a definite knowledge *(sampratyaya)* resting on the remainder after the elimination of certain possible objects *(prasaktapratiśedha)* because of the irrelevance in the case of other objects *(anyatra aprasamgāt)*[33]. For example, sound has been characterized as an existent and non eternal, which are the common characteristics of substance, quality and action. So it is being differentiated from *sāmānya, viśeṣya and samavāya* because these are eternal. But when doubt arises whether sound is a substance, quality or action, it can be eliminated like this: sound cannot be a substance because it inheres in a singular substance *(eka-dravyatvāt)*. It cannot be an action because it is the cause of another sound *(Śabdāntarahetutvāt)*. What remains is quality. Therefore, sound can be regarded as a quality[34]. *Sāmānyotadṛṣṭa* inference is that in which the relation between the probans and probandum *(liṅgaliṅginosambadha)* is being imperceptible *(apratyakṣya)* and the imperceptible probandum *(apratyakṣoliṅgi)* is inferred from similarity *(sāmānyāt)* of the probans to something else[35]. Let's have an example, the self *(ātmā)* is inferred from desire etc., because desire etc. are qualities and qualities always inhere in substance. Therefore, the self is the substratum of qualities like desire etc.

However, these are clear indications of a form of *parārthānumāna.*

**Member's of syllogism : Avayavas are ascertained by *pramāṇas***

*Vātsyāyana* holds that the four inferential components like *pratijñā* etc., are ascertained by the four instruments of valid knowledge mentioned by Gotama. As a matter of fact, the components of inference, without being based on instruments of valid knowledge, cannot ascertain any truth. Therefore, he holds that the inference-components like *pratijñā* etc. are ascertained by four *pramāṇas,* like perception etc, such as: *pratijñā* or declaration of statements is verbal understanding *(āgama)* because 'what is going to be established has been declared' i.e. 'the mountain is fiery'. The probans or *hetu* for the establishment of the proposition is inference *(anumāna)* i.e. 'because there is smoke'. The *udāharaṇa* or example is perception like 'where there is smoke there is fire, like kitchen'. *Upanaya* or application is comparison i.e. in the kitchen the smoke was pervaded by fire and here there is same smoke (i.e. it is also pervaded by fire). And *nigamana* or conclusion is a demonstration of the result of all these *pratijñā*[36] etc. *Vātsyāyana* calls it *paramo nyāyaḥ* or *Nyāya* par excellence[37].

*Pratijñā,* as *sūtrakāra* defined, is a declaration of what is going to be proved *(sādhyanirdeśaḥ)*. But it does not satisfy all necessary conditions. Therefore, *Vātsyāyana* clarifies it extending the definition little further. *Pratijñā,* as he defines, is a proposition stating a specified subject as qualified by the characteristics sought to be proved[38].

## Avayavas as per *Vātsyāyana*

The nuclear sense to be noted is that *Vātsyāyana* has used the word *sādhya* in the sense of *pakṣa*[39]. He also keeps the meaning of *hetu* unchanged. However, from his explanation of *hetu* it can be easily concluded that there are of two divisions of probans such as *anvayin* and *vyatirekin*[40] (both are dependent on the nature of *vyāpti). Vātsyāyana* has no second voice regarding the third, fourth and fifth member of syllogism i.e. *udāharaṇa, upanaya* and *nigamana* respectively. *Vātsyāyana* also accepts five kinds of *hetvābhāsas* without any objection. He then just expands the definition of those fallacious reasons with their respective examples.

However, both the philosophers i.e. Gotama and *Vātsyāyana* have not mentioned anything about *parāmarśa.* but they certainly have put the idea that has been discovered in the later period.

## Theory of inference according to *Nyāyavārttika*: Appeared in a challenging period

The process of inference has been developed gradually in the course of time. In between the Buddhist logicians interacted and criticized, which helped *Naiyāyikas* a lot to develop their system in a proper manner. Udyotakara[41], a man of logic wrote a sub-commentary on *Nyāyasūtra*. He appeared by the time when the Buddhist logicians such as: *Dignāga* and *Dharmakirtī* were challenging the system.

**Udyotakara on *Nyāyasūtra***

Udyotakara takes each and every word of *Nyāyasūtra* 1.1.5 and defines it. The first word is *'atha'*, which has been defined by him, as sequence or continuity[42]. It means after defining *pratyakṣa sūtrakāra* proceeds to define *anumāna*. The very idea of doing so is that the word *'atha'* carries more than one meaning such as: *maṅgala, anantara, ārambha, praśna and kārtsnya*[43]. Here, he adopts the meaning *'anantara'*. Then he takes the word *'tat-pūrvakaṃ'* where he gives three alternative explanations[44]. The word *'tat-pūrvakaṃ'*, as per his first explanation, stands for all forms of valid knowledge *(tat-pūrvakaṃ)*. This explanation of Udyotakara declares that all means of valid knowledge (including that of inference and verbal understanding as well) is preceeded by it. This also does not go against *Bhāṣya's* declaration that 'inference proceeds from perception', because all means of valid knowledge are indirectly dependent on perception. Second explanation is *tat-pūrvakaṃ* and the meaning that it signifies is only 'perception'. And the third explanation is *'te-pūrvakaṃ'* means perceptions, which represents two perceptions by two premises such as *liṅga-liṅgisambandha darśana* (perception of the relation between the probans and the probandum) and *liṅgadarśanaṃ* (i.e. perception of probans).

This second perception awakens the impression left by the former perception, which leads to remember the relation between the probans and the probandum. And after this remembrance, when the probans will be perceived the third perception of the probans with former two perceptions along with remembrance gives birth to the inferential cognition, which is known as *parāmarśa*[45]. This process of inference follows four steps such as:

**The process in nutshell**

1) perception of the relation of probans and the probandum (in the kitchen etc.) -------> first perception
2) perception of the probans somewhere in the mountain -------> second perception
3) perception of probans as invariably concomitant with its probandum -------> third perception
4) inferential cognition -------> the result

Here, it is pretty clear that the concept of *parāmarśa* has been introduced for the first time by Udyotakara. The later logicians developed this notion of *parāmarśa* further. The third alternative explanation of the word *'tat-pūrvakaṃ'* denotes the notion of the remembrance of the relation of probans and the probandum. So, that which is preceded by the remembrance of the relation of probans and probandum is called *anumāna*. Here, he has introduced the concept of *liṅgaparāmarśa*,.[46]

We can summarize above three explanations in this way. The first one says that inference not only directly preceded by perception but stands for all forms of valid knowledge. The second explanation conveys the meaning like inference is produced by perception only. Whereas, the third explanation holds that the inference is the recognition of invariable concomitance between *hetu* and *pakṣa*, which (recognition) is called *liṅgaparāmarśa*.

***Liṅgaparāmarśa is anumāna***

Now the question arises like 'what type of *anumana* is this?' Is it the remembrance of the relation between the probans and the probandum. Or is it the perception of the probans?[47] To which several answers have been given such as: Some people explain that it (inference) is the remembrance of the relation between the probans and probandum [48]. Some people hold that this remembrance as the means, but only in so far as it is aided by the perception of the relation of the probans and the probandum and such other functions[49]. A third party considers that *liṅgaparāmarśa* (the probans as invariably concomitant with the probandum) is the inference[50]. Keeping all these discussions in mind Udyotakara gives his own statement. He holds that in case of inference all these factors are necessary, because they all play an equal role in the process. But among these factors the last one i.e. *liṅga-parāmarśa* seems to be most important, because we find that the inferential cognition of the probandum follows immediately after *parāmarśa*[51].

Thus, Udyotakara emphasizes on *parāmarśa,* more precisely, on *liṅgaparāmarśa.*

**The division : Division based on the nature of *hetu***

Udyotakara now turns to the part of the *sūtra,* which says that inference is of three kinds. First of all he divides inference on the basis of the nature of *hetu.* This type of division is neither seen in *Nyāyasūtra* nor in *Nyāyabhāṣya.* Those inferences are *anvayi anumāna* (positive inference), *vyatireki anumāna* (negative inference) and *anvayivyatireki anumāna* (positive and negative inference)[52]. The positive inference occurs there where the probans exists in association with probandum in the inferential subject *(pakṣa)* but not in *vipakṣa*[53]. For example, sound is non-eternal because it is a product. Here, it has no dissimilar example. In the case of negative inference the probans exists in the subject in which case there is nothing apart from the subject in which the probandum is known to exist. And which *(hetu)* does not exist where the probandum is known to be absent[54]. For example, 'the living body is not soul-less because, it is associated with life'. The third one i.e. positive-negative inference suggests that where there is probans there is probandum and where there is absence of probans there is absence of probandum[55]. For example, sound is non-eternal, because while belonging to a generality and being possessed of specified individuality, it is perceived by the external organs of ordinary human life like us.

**Udyotakara on threefold division of *Vātsyāyana***

After defining three-fold inference of his own now he proceeds to define the three-fold division of inference given by *Vātsyāyana*. He defines it in a different manner. The word *'pūrva'* means probandum and *pūrvavat* means which invariably have the probandum for its probans[56]. Similarly, the word *'śeṣa'* stands for the probandum and other things related to it. So, that which has the probandum and its related things for its probans, is called *śeṣavat*[57]. The very difference here is that the former is invariably concomitant with the probandum only. Whereas, the later is invariably concomitant with the probandum as well as to the things related to it (probans). And *sāmānyatodṛṣṭānumāna* is that in which an object is cognized as qualified by a character which is an invariable concomitant of a well-known character of that object, the former character being independent of the notion of the cause and effect relationship. For example, the presence of water is inferred from the presence of swans[58]. However, the idea of inferring from the motion of sun has not been accepted by him, because there can not be any *hetu* for this. Udyotakara strongly discards the alternative definition of inference[59]. According to him, effect can not be inferred from the cause because no man in his senses is ever found to cognize the effect on seeing the cause[60].

***Trividha* stands for the classification of *hetu***

Udyotakara gives another explanation of the word *'trividha'* which is based on the nature and function of hetu. According to him, the word *'trividha'* does not stand for the division of *anumana* but for the classification of *hetu*. Three kinds of hetus are well known, true and certain[61]. That which is concomitant with the subject is called 'well known probans' or *prasiddha hetu*[62]. The probans that which is concomitant with the subject and in the things similar to that is called true probans or *sadhetu*[63]. And that which never found apart from things of same kind is called *sandigdha hetu*[64]. He also gives another alternative explanation of the word *'trividha'*. The word *'trividha'*, as he suggests, may be taken to restrict the number of inferences[65]. However, according to him, there are endless divisions of inference[66]. Hence, to restrict these the *sūtra* speaks of three kinds.

**Members of syllogism:**

Udyotakara gives a clear definition of *avayavayas*. He holds *avayavayas* or factors of reasoning as a statement which forms part of inferential argument[67]. So, the definition of *avayavayas,* as has been given by Udyotakara, follows like this. 'Those factors of reasoning, which serve to accomplish a purpose not accomplished by other, and which, through these purposes combine together in the focus of a single compound sentence, and thus collectively accomplish the one desired purpose of proving the conclusion to the other party'[68].

Udyotakara also accepts a syllogism containing five members. He then just elaborates the idea of *Vātsyāyana*. Of course, there is a rigorous debate between *Nayiyāyikas* and Buddhist logicians regarding the definition of *pratijñā*. The other members of syllogism like *hetu, udāharaṇa, upanaya* and *nigamana* have been discussed at length by him. However, no difference of opinion with *bhāṣya* has been seen.

**Hetvābhāsa : The number of hetvābhāsas**

Udyotakara gives a full-fledged definition of *hetvābhāsa*. Those are fallacious probans because they don't posses all the characteristics of a good *hetu* but are sufficient enough to appear as such[69]. So, it doesn't satisfy all the necessary characteristics of a good reason but it appears to be so. He then proceeds to define the numbers of *hetvābhāsas*. It's number, as he suggests, is more than five. On one hand their number cannot be calculated *(ananta),* but in other hand, more precisely, their number goes to 176. He suggests this number on the basis of the diversities of time, person and the thing to be proved[70]. There are sixteen cases where the *sādhya* pervades the *hetu*[71]. A similar list of sixteen arises where *hetu* pervades of only a part of *sādhya*[72], and another sixteen occurs where *hetu* is absent from *sādhya*[73]. Finally, the number of *hetvābhāsa,* as has been accepted by the system, is five.

**Difference with Bhāṣya**

Udyotakara gives an alternate definition of *Viruddha hetvābhāsa.* It occurs, according to him, when either the reason contradicts the hypothesis or hypothesis contradicts the reason[74]. For example, "sound is eternal, because it is a product". He further proceeds to discuss *sādhyasama* or *asiddha hetvābhāsa.* Here he classifies it into three such *as prajñāpaniyadharmasamāna (Vācaspati Miśra* calls it *svarūpāsiddha), āsrayāsiddha* and *anyathāsiddha hetvābhāsa*[75]. The first one occurs where the *hetu* is as much as in need of proof as *sādhya.* Second one occurs where the locus or substratum *(āśrya)* of *hetu* is not known and in the case of third one the *hetu* can be explained in such way *(anyathā)* which would make it a proof. A befitting example for it is "shadow is a substance because it has motion".

Thus, Udyotakara has developed the idea of inference in his commentary on *Nyāyabhāṣya.*

**Theory of inference according to *Nyāyavārttikatātparyaṭīkā***

The science *(śāstra),* which is the cause of liberation of mankind, was composed by *Akṣapāda* and explained by

*Pakṣilasvāmi.* Apart from this Udyotakara wrote *vārttika* because people were misled by the bad reasoings of logicians like *Dignāga* etc[76]. This is the opening statement of *Vācaspati Miśra,* the writer of *Tātparyaṭikā* on *Nyāyavārttika.* His time, as has been fixed by the philosophers, is a matter of controversial issue. However, it is fmally accepted that he lived in between 900-980 A.D. approximately.[77]

*Vācaspati Miśra* flourished in a quiet developed stage of *Nyāya* system. His effort on *Nyāyasūtra* is known as *Nyāyavārttikatātparyaṭikā.* A valid cognition, according to *Vācaspati Miśra,* is invariably associated with its object, because it produces activities that are successful. In other words, after knowing an object our activity, with regard to that object, proceeds successfuIly[78].

A question, rcgarding the validity of inference, was put forth by the Buddhist logicians. "If the inference is not valid", replies *Vācaspati Miśra,* "then either we may invite a vicious circle by trying to prove the validity of inference by another inference. Or we may fail to express a meaningful proposition unless we admit verbal understanding as a separate source of cognition apart from perception"[79].

## Vācaspati Miśra on Nyāyasūtra

*Vācaspati Miśra* has not prepared any new definition for inference. Rather he claims that the definition of inference, such as *'tat-pūrvakaṃ'* suffers from the narrow application as well as over application[80]. Because from the word *'tat'* perception is implied. It means inference is preceded by perception. If it is so then verbal testimony etc. can be regarded as inference because these are also preceded by perception. This is the case of over application[81]. Secondly, if somebody first infers fire and then he proceeds to infer the hotness of the inferred fire then in that case this definition of inference will not work (because the later inference is not preceded by perception). This case, in philosophical language, is called narrow application of the definition[82]. Therefore, keeping all problems in view, he dissolves the compound *'tatpūrvakaṃ'* in three alternative ways.

First of all he delives the meaning as *'tāni'* of the word *'tat'*[83]. By doing so he includes not only perception but all *pramāṇas* also. His second alternative explanation conveys meaning like 'that which is preceded by two perceptions'. Here, he explains the terms like *Vāstyāyana.* Similar thing happens in the case of third explanation also.

*Vācaspati Miśra* opines that the example of *sāmānya-todṛṣṭānumāna,* cited by the commentator, is not fit to the context. According to him, this example comes under *śeṣavat* inference because here also from the change of the place of sun the motion of sun can be inferred[84]. *Sāmānyato-dṛṣṭānumāna,* as he explains, is the inference of probandum *(dharmī),* which is seen to be invariably connected *(avin-ābhāva)* with the probans[85]. For example, the place known as with cranes is the means of inference of the place as with water. However, he supports Udyotakara in the context of endless division of inference.

He has explained the word *'trividha'* of inference on the basis of five characteristics of *hetu*, which are classed under following three heads such as *śeṣavat, sāmānyatodṛṣṭa* and *śeṣavatsāmānyatodṛṣṭa*[86]. Again the number of *hetvā-bhāsa,* as given by him, is 2032[87].

*Vācaspati Miśra,* while defining the subdivisions of *hetvā-bhāsa,* says *savyabhicāra* and *aneikāntika* are synonymous. Therefore, one can be used as a definition of the other[88]. He divides *sādhyasama hetvābhāsa* into four varieties keeping three varieties of Udyotakara unchanged. The additional one is known as *ekadeśāsiddha.* It occurs when the *hetu* is partially absent from the inferential subject i.e. *pakṣa*[89]. *Vācaspati*

*Miśra* is not satisfied with the explanation of *kālātyayāpadiṣṭa hetvābhāsa* given by *Vātsyāyana* and Udyotakara[90].

However, in this way *Vācaspati Miśra* has depicted the process of inference.

**Theory of inference according to *Nyāyavārttikatātparyaṭikāpariśuddhi (NVTTP)***

The main objective of Udayana in writing *pariśuddhi* was the exposition of the views of *Vācaspati Miśra,* the author of *Tātparyaṭikā*[91]. *Pariśuddhi* is a commentary on *Tātparyaṭikā.* When *Vācaspati Miśra* was criticized by a host of Buddhist logicians, Udayana, better known as *Ācārya,* flourished to protect him from those *kutārkikas.* In the language of Anantalal Thakur it is written as "... Udayana is the last great master of ancient *Nyāya* and is, according to many, the priest of that fertile marriage between *Nyāya* and *Vaiśeṣika* which gave birth to Navya *Nyāya*"[92]. His time, as has been fixed by Frauwallner, falls in between 1050 to 1100 A.D.[93].

However, as he declared to follow *Vācaspati Miśra* strictly. So he did. Hence his theory of inference carries no difference of opinion with comparison to the theory of *Vācaspati Miśra.* Therefore, there is no need of explaining it further.

**Theory of inference according to *Nyāyamañjarī: Nyāyamañjarī* a mature sanskrit work of Indian logic**

Apart from the tradition of writing sub-commentaries on commentaries we have a tradition of writing independent commentary on *Nyāyasūtra. Nyāyamañjarī,* a mature sanskrit work on Indian logic, is of this kind. Its authorship is ascribed to a *Kashmirian Brahman, Jayanta Bhaṭṭa* by name. He seems to appear after Udyotakara and before *Vācaspati Miśra.* Hence his time, as approximately has been fixed by Steinkellener, is 840 to 900 A.D.[94]. Needless to say that a good deal of controversy has been entertained with this regard. However, this author is famous for his independent views.

*Pramāṇa,* according to *Jayanta Bhaṭṭa,* is a collection of two types of entities like conscious and unconscious[95]. This collection, otherwise called *pramāṇa,* produces the cognition of an object, which is other than illusion and doubt. This *pramāṇa,* which has been considered as an instrument of valid knowledge[96], is of four kinds. *Nyāyamañjarī* forms a chapter on inference where five subsections have been presented. Those are as follows.

1) the fivefold nature of probans[97]
2) the problem of invariable concomitance[98]
3) justification of the validity of inference[99]
4) the *Nyāyasūtra* definition of inference[100]
5) the cognition of time and space[101]

However, the way *Jayanta Bhaṭṭa* defines *anumāna* is neither seen in the commentary of *Vātsyāyana* nor in the sub-commentary of Udyotakara. In his language, inference is the cognition relating to the probandum *(liṅgin jñānam)* not in contact in sense organ *(parokṣa),* which appears when the probans fulfilling a fivefold nature *(pañcalakṣakāliṅgāt)* and there is a recollection of relevant relation called invariable concomitance between probans and the probandum *(gṛdhitānniyamasmṛteḥ)*[102]. In this case the knowledge of the probans along with the meaning of invariable concomitance acts as *pramāṇa* and the knowledge of probandum acts as the result of that *pramāṇa*[103]. However, from his explanation of inference following steps can be noted.

1) the perception of probans (which fulfills five essential characteristics)
2) recollection of the relation between probans and probandum

3) inferential cognition

Hence, it is clear that *Jayanta Bhaṭṭa* does not employ the factor called *parāmarśa* in the precess of inference. He considers it saying, "the first step is the perception of reason, then the remembrance of universal concomitancc. The third step is, according to some, the knowledge of confirmatory cognition"[104]. The above discussion clearly states that he does not require any component called *parāmarśa.* Without this component, as he records, the *upanaya,* the fourth member of the syllogism, can be established[105].

After defining *anumana* in the above-mentioned way Jayanta *Bhaṭṭa* comes forward to define the structural analysis of the *Nyāyasūtra*. According to him, the word *'tat-pūrvakaṃ'* constitutes the definition of inference. *'Tat'* is a pronoun here; it signifies the perception, which is implied from the context[106]. He holds that this pronoun *'tat'* is in dual number (two perceptions). It also does not create any problem to include comparison etc. One perception discovers the relation of universal concomitance while the other perception discovers the presence of the reason in the subject of inference[107].

Jayanta *Bhaṭṭa* now analyzes the division of inference. A *śeṣavat anumāna,* as *Vātsyāyana* describes, is the case of inference of effect from its cause as in the case of inferring rain from the current of the river. But it is not right, says Jayanta *Bhaṭṭa,* because it may be the case that the rain (or effect) occurs somewhere in the upper part of the country and swift current of the river is seen due to its connection with the lower part of the same country[108]. Therefore, the cause is inferred from its effect is merely a verbal testimony. But what is in reality is that the subject of the inference plays the part of the consequence as well as that of reason as it has different aspects[109]. And *sāmānyatodṛṣṭa* inference occurs where we infer the result from the reason, which is neither a cause nor an effect[110]. For example, the list of a wood apple is inferred from its color etc. Here color and taste inheres in a wood apple but not causally related to each other[111].

Jayanta *Bhaṭṭa* takes the credit of introducing the two fold division of inference such as *svārtha* and *parārtha* to the *Nyāya* system. This tradition of dividing inference has been originated from *Praśastapāda*, the commentator of *Vaiśeṣikasūtra*. In the language of C.D. Bijalwan "Jayanta has the credit of introducing these two types in the *Nyāya* and thereby initializing a new tradition so far not accepted in this school"[112]. On the other hand, he does not accept the three-fold division of inference such as *Kevalānvayi* etc[113].

Jayanta *Bhaṭṭa* follows Gautama in the context of describing the fallacious reasons. He gives a detailed study of all the five types and sub types of *hetvābhāsas* with a nomenclature.

**The Conclusion:**

The above discussion of inference helps us to find out a good deal of notable points. Inference keeps on changing its form starting from *Vātsyāyana* to Udayana. Udyotakara gives a finishing touch to it introducing a concept called *parāmarśa,* which has been widely accepted by the new logicians. Jayanta introduces the twofold division of inference i.e. *svārtha* and *parārtha* to the system, on which the *Navya Nyāya* tradition of Indian logic is greatly dependent.

## FOOTNOTES

1. He is also known as *Gautama, Akṣapāda, Dirghatapas* etc. as it is ascribed in various scriptures.
2. Vide. N.S. 1.1.1 प्रमाणप्रमेयसंशय.....तत्त्वज्ञानान्निःश्रेयसाधिगमः
3. Vide. N.S. 1.1.3 प्रत्यक्षानुमानोपमानश्शब्दाः प्रमाणानि।
4. N.S.1.1.5 अथ तत्पूर्वकं त्रिविधमनुमानम्...।
5. N.S. 2.1.38 रोधोपघातसादृश्येभ्यो व्यभिचारादनुमानप्रमाणम्।

6 N.S. 1.1.5 पूर्ववच्छेषवत्सामान्यतोदृष्टं च।

7. Vide, N.S. 1.1.32 प्रतिज्ञाहेतूदाहरणोपनयनिगमनान्यवयवा:।

8. Ibid. 1.1. 34/35

9. Vide, N.S. 1.1.36 उदहारणसाधर्म्यात्साध्यसाधनं हेतु।

10. Vide N.S. 1.1.38

11. Vide N.S. 1.1.39 हेत्वपदेशात्प्रतिज्ञाया: पुनर्वचनं निगमनम्।

12. Vide N.S. 1.1.1.

13. Vide N.S. 1.2.4. सव्यभिचारविरुद्धप्रकरणसमसाध्यसमकालातीता हेत्वाभासा:

14. Vide N.S. 1.2.5. अनैकान्तिक: सव्यभिचार:।

15. Vide N.S. 1.2.6. सिद्धान्तमभ्युपेत्य तद्विरोधी विरुद्ध:।

16. Vide N.S. 1.2.7.

17. Vide N.S. 1.2.8.

18. Vide N.S. 1.2.9. कालात्ययापदिष्ट: कालातीत:।

19. EIP, p. 129

20. Ibid.

21. NS, p. xiii

22. NBh. Opening statement प्रमाणतोऽर्थप्रतिपतौ प्रवृत्तिसामर्थ्यात्।

23. NBh. 1.1.3 मितेनलिङ्गेन लिङ्गिनोऽर्थस्य पश्चात्मानम्।

24. Ibid. 1.1.5 तत्पूर्वकमित्ययेन लिङ्गतिङ्गिनो: सम्बन्धदर्शनं चाऽभिसमबध्यते।

25. ibid

26. *Viśwanātha's vṛtti* on N.S. 1.1.5.

27. NBh. 1.1.5 पूर्ववत्–यत्र कारणेन कार्यमनुमीयते।

28. ibid. शेषवत्–यत्र कार्येण कारणमनुमीयते।

29. ibid. सामान्यतोदृष्टम्–व्रज्यापूर्वकमन्यत्र दृष्टस्याऽन्यत्र दर्शनमिति।

30. NBh. 1.1.5

31. AP, p. 69

32. NBh. 1.1.5 यत्र यथापूर्वं प्रत्यक्षभूतयोऽन्यतरस्याऽप्रत्यक्षस्यनुमानम्।

33. Ibid. स च प्रसक्तप्रतिषेधेऽन्यत्राऽप्रसिद्धाच्छिष्यमाणे सम्प्रत्यय:।

34. Ibid.

35. Ibid. यत्राऽप्रत्यक्षे लिङ्गलिङ्गिनो: सम्बन्धे केनचिदर्थेन लिङ्गस्य समान्यादप्रत्यक्षो लिङ्गी गम्यते।

36. Ibid. तेषु प्रमाणसमवाय: आगम: प्रतिज्ञा, हेतुरनुमानम्, उदाहरणं प्रत्यक्षम्। उपनयमुपमानम्, सर्वेषामेकार्थसमवाये सामर्थ्यदर्शनं निगमनमिति।

37. NBh.1.1.1
38. NBh. 1.1.1. प्रज्ञापनीयेन धर्मेण धर्मिणो विशिष्टस्य परिग्रहवचनं प्रतिज्ञा।
39. *Nyāya* Philosophy by Debiprasad and *Mṛnālakānti,* p. 107
40. AP, p. 87
41. He is also known as *Bharadvāja, Pāśupatācārya.* HIL, p. 124
42. NV 1.1.5 अथेत्यानन्तर्ये।
43. *Amarakośa*—मङ्गलानन्तराम्भप्रश्नकात्स्न्यष्वथो अथ।
44. NV 1.1.5 तानि ते तत् पूर्वं यस्य तदिदं तत्पूर्वकम्।
45. Ibid. बुभुत्सावतो द्वितीयलिङ्गदर्शनात् संस्काराभिव्यक्त्युत्तरकालं स्मृतिः, स्मृत्यनन्तरं च पुनर्लिङ्गदर्शनमयं धूम इति। तदिदमन्तिमं प्रत्यक्षं पूर्वाभ्यां प्रत्यक्षाभ्यां स्मृत्या चानुगृह्यमाणां परामर्शरूपानुमानं भवति।
46. Ibid..... तत्पूर्वं यस्य तदिदं तत्पूर्वकमिति......लिङ्गलिङ्गिसम्बन्धदर्शनान्तरलिङ्ग-दर्शनसम्बन्धस्मृतिभिर्लिङ्गपरामर्शो विशिष्यते।
47. Ibid. लिङ्गलिङ्गिसम्बन्धस्मृतिर्लिङ्गदर्शनं वा इति सन्देहः।
48. NV 1.1.5 एके तावद्वर्णयन्ति लिङ्गलिङ्गिसम्बन्धस्मृतिरनुमानम्।
49. Ibid. इतरैलिङ्गलिङ्गिसम्बन्धदर्शनादिभिरनुगृह्यमाणा।
50. अपरे तु मन्यन्ते लिङ्गपरामर्शादनुमानम्—Ibid.
51. Ibid. वयं तु पश्यामः—सर्वमनुमानम्, अनुमितेस्तन्नान्तरीयकत्वात्। प्रधानोपसर्जनता-विवक्षयां लिङ्ग, परामर्श इति न्याय्यम्।
52. NV 1.1.5 त्रिविधमिति। अन्वयी व्यतिरेकी अन्वयव्यतिरेकी चेति।
53. Ibid. अन्वयी विवक्षिततज्जातीयवृत्तित्वे सति विपक्षहीन।
54. Ibid. व्यतिरेकी विवक्षितव्यापकत्वे सति सपक्षाभावे सति विपक्षावृत्तिः।
55. Ibid. अन्वयीव्यतिरेकी विवक्षिततज्जातीयोपपत्तौ विपक्षावृत्तिः।
56. NV 1.1.5 पूर्वं साध्यम्, तद्व्याप्त्या यस्यास्तीति तत् पूर्ववत्।
57. NV 1.1.5 साध्यतज्जातीयः शेषः, तद्यस्यास्तीति तत् शेषवत्।
58. Ibid. सामान्यतोदृष्टं नाम आकार्याकारणीभूतेन यत्राविनाभाविना विशेषणेन विशेष्यमाणो धर्मी गम्यते तत्।
59. EIP, p. 311
60. NV 1.1.5 न हि कारणं गृहीत्वा स्वस्यात्मा कश्चित् कार्यं प्रतिपद्यत इति तथा च व्याहतं भवति।
61. NV 1.1.5 अथवा त्रिविधमिति लिङ्गस्य प्रसिद्धसदसन्दिग्धतामाह।
62. Ibid. प्रसिद्धमिति पक्षे व्यापकम्।

63. Ibid. सदिति सजातोयेऽस्ति।
64. Ibid. सन्दिग्धमिति सजातीयाविनीभावि।
65. अथवा त्रिविधमिति नियमार्थम्।
66. Ibid. तस्य त्वान्तर्गणिकोऽनन्तभेद इति।
67. NV 1.1.32 वाक्याङ्गत्वमवयवार्थः।
68. Ibid. परप्रतिपादका ये वाक्याङ्गभूता इतरेतराप्रत्यायितेनार्थेनार्थवन्तो वाक्याङ्गतामुपयान्ति तेऽवयवाः।
69. NV 1.2.4 हेतुलक्षणाभावादहेतवो हेतुसामान्याद्धेतुवदाभासमानाः–हेत्वाभसाः।
70. Ibid. काल-पुरुष-वस्तुभेदानुविधानेनापरिसंङ्खेयः, सामान्यतः साध्यवस्तूपग्रहेण हेतुहेत्वाभासाभेदः प्रपञ्चमानः षट्सप्ततिशतम्।
71. Ibid. तत्र साध्यव्यापकधर्मभेदः षोडशधा।
72. Ibid. साध्यैकदेशवृत्तिधर्मोऽप्येवम्।
73. Ibid. एवं साध्यवृत्तिधर्मभेदः।
74. NV 1.2.6 यदा प्रज्ञाया हेतुविरोधो हेतोर्वा प्रतिज्ञाविरोधकत्वं तदा विरुद्धो हेतुरिति।
75. NV 1.2.8 सोऽयमसिद्धस्त्रेधा भवति–प्रज्ञापनीयधर्मसमान, आश्रयासिद्धः अन्यथा-सिद्धश्चेति।
76. NVTT opening statement अथ भगवताऽक्षपादेन निश्रेयहेतौ शास्त्रे प्रणीते, व्युत्पादिते च भगवता पक्षिलस्वामिना....सूत्रकारोक्तप्रयोजनानुवादपूर्वकं वार्त्तिक-कारम्भप्रयोजनं दर्शयति।
77. EIP, p. 10
78. NVTT 1.1.1
79. Ibid.
80. NVTT 1.1.5 तस्मादव्याप्त्यतिव्याप्तिभ्यामलक्षणमेतदित्यत आह।
81. Ibid.
82. Ibid.
83. NVTT 1.1.5 तत्र प्रथमे विग्रहे तानीत्यनन्तरंसूत्रमुलंध्य विभागसूत्रगताः प्रत्यक्षादयः संबन्धनीयाः, योग्यत्वात्।
84. NVTT 1.1.5 सामान्यतोदृष्टोदाहरणं भाष्यकारीयं दुरवबोधं शेषवदुदाहरणान्तर्गत च।
85. Ibid. अत्रापि कार्येण सवितुर्देशान्तरप्राप्त्या तत्कारणस्य ब्रज्याया अनुमानम्।
86. Ibid. सामान्यनाविनाभाविना हेतुना लक्षितं दृष्टं धर्मिरूपमनुनानं सामान्यतो-दृष्टमनुमानम्।
87. NVTT 1.2.4 तदेवं प्रकृतिभूताष्टचत्वारिंशत् प्रक्षेपेण सम्पिण्डितं द्वित्रिंशे द्वे सहस्त्रे भवतः इति।
88. AP, p. 108

89. Vide NVTT 1.2.8
90. AP, p. 108
91. NVTTP *Maṅgalācaraṇaṃ* वाचस्पतेर्वचसि न स्खलतो यथैते।
92. NVTTP edited by Anantalal Thakur, lCPR, New Delhi, Introductory passage.
93. EIP, p. 10
94. EIP, p. 9
95. NM on *sūtra* 1.1.3 बोधाबोधस्वभावा सामग्री प्रमाणम्।
96. Ibid. करणसाधनोऽयं प्रमाणशब्दः।
97. Ibid. लिङ्गशब्दनिर्वचनं, तस्य पञ्चलक्षणं च।
98. Ibid तादात्म्यतदुत्पतिभ्यां व्याप्तिनिरूपणम्।
99. Ibid. अनुमानलक्षणोपेक्षसमाधानम्।
100. Ibid. तत्पूर्वकं इत्येतावदेव लक्षणपरम्।
101. Ibid.
102. NM 1.1.5 पञ्चलक्षणकाल्लिङ्गात् गृहितान्नियमस्मृतेः।
परोक्षे लिङ्गिनि ज्ञानं अनुमानं प्रचक्षते।।
103. Ibid. अत्र लिङ्ग-विषयं ज्ञानंविषयीकृतं वा लिङ्गप्रतिबन्धस्मरणसहितं प्रमाणम्। लिङ्गज्ञानं फलम्।
104. Ibid. अत्र प्रथमं लिङ्गदर्शनं, ततः प्रतिबन्धस्मरणं, ततः केषाञ्चिन्मते परामर्शज्ञानं, ततः साध्यार्थप्रतीतिः।
105. Ibid. येषामपि मते परामर्शज्ञानं नास्ति तैरप्युनयवचनमवश्यमेवापरिहार्यमनुमेय प्रतिपत्तये।
106. NM 1.1.5 न च कारणेन कार्यमनुमातुमपि पार्यते। कार्यस्य तावत् पक्षत्वमयुक्तम्। तदिति सर्वनाम्ना प्रकान्तं प्रत्यक्षमवमृश्यते।
107. Ibid. एतावत्युच्चमाने निर्णयोपमानादौ तत्पूर्वके प्रसङ्गो न वायावर्तत इति तद्व्यावृत्तये द्विवचनान्तेन विग्रहः प्रदर्शयितव्यः।
108. NM 1.1.5 अयं देशो वा वृष्टिविशिष्टदेशान्तरसंसृष्टः विशिष्टनदीपूरवत्त्वेनानुमीयत इति.....नास्ति प्रसरः।
109. Ibid. परमार्थतस्तु धर्मीधर्मवत्त्वेन धर्मवाननुमीयत इति स्थितिः।
110. Ibid. यत् अकार्यकारणभूताल्लिङ्गात् तादृस्यैव लिङ्गिनोऽनुमानम्।
111. Ibid. रूपरसयोः समवायिकारणमेकं कपित्थादिद्रव्यम्, न तु तयोरन्योन्यं कार्यकारणभावः।
112. ITK, p.142
113. Ibid., p.143

# CHAPTER-V
# THEORY OF INFERENCE ACCORDING TO NAVYA NYĀYA

## General Background

"A close dialogue", says Prof. V.N. Jha, "with the *Buddhist* logicians and philosophers generated remarkable structural depths in classical Indian philosophical thoughts. The experience of this dialogue generated the necessity of formulating a language of precise communication. This gave birth to the *Navya-nyāya* language"[1]. The above statement of Prof. Jha briefs the necessity of developing a tradition, which provides the language of precise communication. The other alternative asset of this tradition is its method of clarification *(pariṣkārapaddhati)*. It leaves no ambiguity. This is the only cause for which all the prominent schools of Indian philosophy adopted this language for the purpose of communication.

Historically, this tradition starts from *Gaṅgeśa,* the author of *Tatvacintāmaṇi* (1200AD). This tradition mainly deals with *pramāṇas*. That's why it is called *pramāṇa-śastra*. However, this chapter aims to discuss the process of inference as it occurs in the *Navya-nyāya* system. The central focus of this chapter will be *Anumānacintāmaṇi* of *Gaṇgeśa*. While doing so, it will keep an eye for the logicians like *Viśwanātha, Annambhaṭṭa and Śaśadhara* etc. In short, this chapter is a chronological study of new-logicians on the concept of inference.

**Knowledge as in Navya-nyāya**

*Navya-nyāya* follows a systematic process of knowledge. First of all, it defines knowledge or *buddhi* as the cause of all our worldly behavior[2]. The word *'vyavahāra'* lies in the definition, expresses thè meaning as 'utter' words for the purpose of communicating ideas,[3]. This *buddhi* cannot be always true, because sometimes we may be misguided by false impressions. Therefore, the system has divided it into two such as remembrance *(smṛiti)* and experience *(anubhava)*[4]. Again, *smṛti* or remembrance cannot satisfy the purpose because this is a product of mental impression[5]. It is just a recollection of a thing, which had been experienced in the past. Now what is left is *anubhava,* which is again twofold like *pramā* or valid knowledge and *apramā* or invalid knowledge. *Apramā* or invalid knowledge is the cognition of a thing not having an attribute, as it seems to possess[6]. For example, the false impression of a snake in a rope. The above definition of *apramā* can be presented in a pictographic form such as:

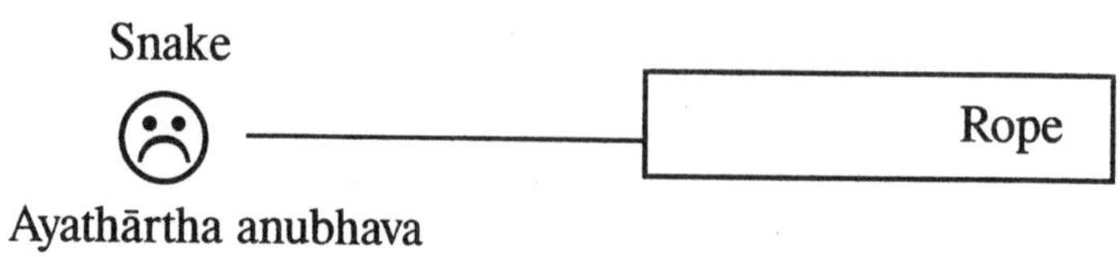


On the other hand, *pramā* or valid knowledge discloses the real nature of the object. The framework of a valid knowledge is greatly dependent on three terms such as *viśeṣ ya, prakāra* and *sambadha*. These three are interdependent. *Prakāra* or adjective is the property of *viśeṣya*. It resides in its locus i.e. *viśeṣya* through a relation *(samambdha)*. Again, this relation is not an ordinary one it is eternal. For example, 'cow'. It is called 'cow' because it has a property called 'cowness'. In other words, 'cow' is qualified by 'cowness'. Here, 'cow' is *viśeṣya,* 'cowness' is *prakāra* and *samambdha* brings them together. This *samambdha* is eternal because without 'cowness' the 'cow' has no existence and vice-versa. However, the present diagram can clear the picture.

Rope

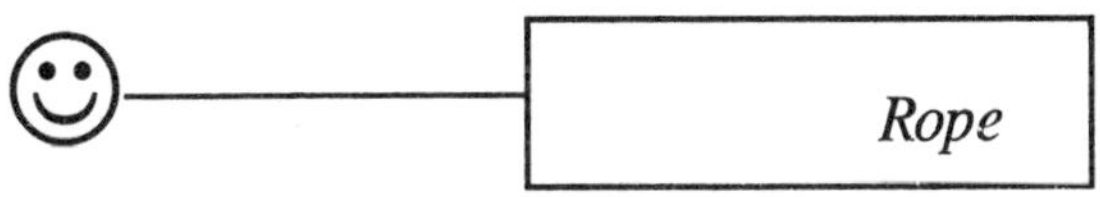


*The real nature of the object (yathārtha anubhava)*

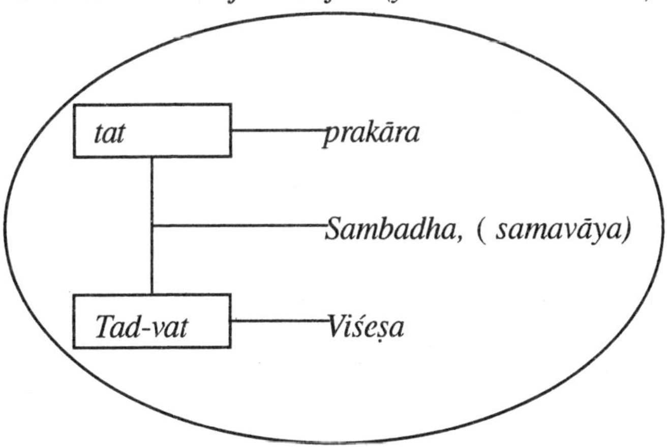


Frame work of a valid knowledge

Again, the system has divided *pramā* into four types like *pratyakṣa, anumiti, upamiti* and *Śābdabodha.* These are the ways of knowing, These *pramāṇas* have their respective instruments *(karaṇa)* and immediate operations *(vyāpāra)* to produce the result such as:

| Kowledge | Instrument | Operation | Result |
|---|---|---|---|
| *Pratyakṣa* | *Indriya* | *Sannikarṣa* | *Pratyakṣya* |
| *Anumāna* | *Vyāptijñāna* | *Parāmarśa* | *Anumiti* |
| *Upamāna* | *Sādṛśya* | *Atideśa-vākya* | *Upamiti* |
| *Śabda* | *Padajñāna* | *Padārthadhī* | *Śābdabodha* |

Among these *pramāṇas* inference stands first because it has a great utility in our everyday life. We cannot perceive each and every object directly but that does not mean that it has no existence. Therefore, for the objects, which are beyond our perception, we employ this process of acquiring knowJedge, which is called *anumāna* or inference.

**The process so far**

Inference, according to *Navya-nyāya,* is the instrument of inferential cognition or *anumiti*. *Anumiti* is produced out of *parāmarśa*[7], wnich has two components like *vyāptijñāna* and *pakṣadharmatājñāna* i.e. *parāmarśa* is the knowledge of the property of the inferential subject *(liṅga),* which is qualified by invariable concomitance[8]. Here, *liṅga* or *hetu* is a thing from which the existence of another thing will be inferred and *vyāpti* is the invariable relationship between the two i.e. the *liṅga* and the *sādhya* (the thing to be inferred). The process goes like this:

| | | |
|---|---|---|
| Step-1: | perception of the *liṅga* | *(hetudarśana)* |
| Step-2: | remembrance of the invariable relationship of *hetu* and *sādhya.* | *(vyāptismaraṇa)* |
| Step-3: | confirmatory cognition | *(parāmarśa)* |
| Step-4: | inferential cognition | *(anumiti)* |

Let us fit the above framework of inference into the stock example of the system i.e. *'parvato vahnimān dhūmāt'* (the mountain has fire, because it has smoke). A person, who has experienced the presence of smoke and fire together in the kitchen, finds a whiff of smoke somewhere in the mountain.

Step-1: *dhūma darśana*

Then, he recollects the universal relationship of smoke and fire (which he had acquired in the past).

Step-2: *vyāptismaraṇa*

After that he combines step-l and step-2 into one like 'the smoke, which exists in the mountain, is qualified by a relationship called invariable concomitance'. This combined knowledge produces a third one called *parāmarśa.*

Step - 1 + step - 2 = step- 3

In the above *process* of inference the intermediate operation *(vyāpāra)* is *parāmarśa.* The knowledge of invariable concomitance acts as instrument[9]. Now, here is a controversy with those Old-logicians. They (Old logicians) hold that the knowledge of invariable concomitance is the immediate operation *(vyāpāra)*[10], whereas, New-logicians substitute *parāmarśa* in its place. Again the old school holds that the *liṅga,* being known[11] as a concomitant, is the instrument of the inference, where as; the new logicians hold the knowledge of invariable concomitance as the instrument of inference[12]. Now let us first definc what is *vyāpāra* and *karaṇa,* then only we will be able to analyze the whole thing.

***Definition of vyāpāra***

The *vyāpāra* or intermediate operation is defined as the knowledge that which is produced by the cause and which produces the effect, which effect was produced by the cause[13]. Here, *'tad'* means instrument. Hence the whole definition follows like this: *'Karaṇajanyatve sati karaṇajanyapha-*

*lajanakatvaṃ*'. Let us apply the above definition into the present context. Here, *karaṇa* is *vyāptijñāna,* so *Vyāptijñāna-janyatve sati vyāptijñānajanyaphala (anumiti) janakatvaṃ.*

**Karaṇa, Its definition and function**

Next comes *karaṇa*. The logicians have interpreted it in two different ways. According to the first interpretation, *karaṇa* should be that cause which is extraordinary and it should possess *vyāpāra (vyāpāravat asādhāraṇa kāraṇaṃ karaṇaṃ).* This is the standpoint of Old logicians. And *karaṇa,* according to new logicians, is the cause, which should not disassociate from its effect *(phalāyogavyavachinna kāraṇaṃ karaṇaṃ).* That means it has to be an immediate connection with the object. But so far the process of inference, carried by new-logicians, the knowledge of *vyāpti* does not lead immediately to a conclusion. In between a component called *parāmarśa* comes to the stage. So the problem, therefore, can be solved, drawing the solution like through such *parāmarśa* or *liṅgapartimārśa* the knowledge of *vyāpti* leads to the conclusion[14].

Thus, the process *of* inference, in general, has been explained in *Navya-nyāya* system of Indian logic.

Inferential cognition, as defined by *Gaṅgeśa,* is the knowledge produced by the knowledge of a Middle term, invariable concomitance with the Major term, exists in the subject[15]. And the instrument of this inferential cognition is inference [16]. This instrumental cause is *liṅgaparāmarśa*[17]. Let us take an example like

The hill has fire,
because it has smoke.

Here, *pakṣadharmatājñāna* (the knowledge that the reason exists in the subject) is the third perception of smoke. And this smoke is not an ordinary smoke. It is qualified by invariable concomitance *(vyāptiviśiṣṭa).* So this *hetu* is invariably associated with *sādhya*. This knowledge is called the instrument *(karaṇa)* of inference. And the knowledge of a middle term pervaded by a major term existing in the subject is the immediate operation *(vyāpāra)*[18]. Here, we find a clear picture of the process of inference. He also brings a clear distinction of *karaṇa* and *vyāpāra*.

Thus, is the process of inference given by *Gaṅgeśa*. *Viśwanātha Pañcānana,* the author of *Nyāyasiddhāntamuktāvalī,* has followed the same process. He holds that in the process of inference the invariable concomitance acts as instrument and *parāmarśa* acts as the intermediate operation[19]. *Annambhaṭṭa,* on the other hand, clarifies the whole thing in his text called *Tarkasaṃgraha* following the method of *Gaṅgeśa.*

We can compare the above process of *Gaṅgeśa, Viśwanātha* and *Annaṃbhaṭṭa* with that of *Śaśadhara,* who appeared after *Ācārya Udayana* but before *Gaṅgeśa.* This study will continue in the second part of this work.

**Elements of inference:**

In the second chapter the general definitions of the components, which are involved in the process of inference, have been discussed. Now I proceed to define these components on the basis of *Navya Naiyāyikas,* especially *Gaṅgeśa.*

***Vyāpti as to Gaṅgeśa***

After establishing the authority of inference, now *Gaṅgeśa* raises the question that 'what is that *vyāpti,* which is the cause of the inferential cognition?[20]. To define *vyāpti* he has given twenty-one tentative definitions, which are traditionally known as provisional definitions *(pūrvapakṣalakṣaṇa)* of *vyāpti* and finally rejects all. Thus, at the end he gives twenty-second definition of *vyāpti,* which is called conclusive definition *(siddhāntalakṣaṇa)*[21]. However, *Navya-naiyāyikas* discuss not only the logical character of *vyāpti* but also the manner of its establishment *(vyāptigrahopāya)*. It is established by the frequent observation of the co-existence of the probans with that of probandum[22].

***Parāmarśa***

The most vital element of inference, as this system regards, is *parāmarśa*. It is defined by *Gaṅgeśa* as the cognition that the subject has probans, which is qualified by the invariable concomitance[23]. In other words, the subject has not the probans merely, but it is invariably related to the probandum. *Viśwanātha* defines *parāmarśa* as the cognition that this mountain has smoke, which is invariably related to the probandum[24]. *Annaṃbhaṭṭa* identifies it (*parāmarśa*) with inference[25]. However, this concept has covered a wider area in this system.

**Hetvābhāsa:**

Logicians have identified some obstructing factors of inference, for which a valid inference cannot be produced. *Navya-naiyāyikas* have defined two types of obstructing factors of inference such as *Hetvābhāsa* and *Udāharaṇābhāsa*[26]. *Gaṅgeśa,* at the very outset of *Hetvābhāsa prakaraṇa,* mentions that by exposing fallacious in the argument of his opponent, one can achieve truth and victory[27]. He gives three alternative definitions of *Hetvābhāsa*[28], express that fallacy is an object of knowledge, which obstructs an inference. *Gaṅgeśa* divides *Hetvābhāsa* into five such as *Savyabhicāra, Viruddha, Satpratipakṣa, Asiddha* and *Bādhita*[29].

*Savyabhicāra* is a probans in which abides a character, the possessor of which causes that presence of two alternatives, which produces doubt in the probandum[30]. This has been sub-divided into three like *Sādhāraṇa, Asādhāraṇa* and *Anupasamhāri*. *Sādhāraṇa* or too-general fallacy abides in the locus of probandum as well as in its absence[31]. For example,

This hill has smoke,

because it has fire.

The *Asādhāraṇa* fallacy abides neither in the locus nor in its absence. For example,

This hill is full of smoke,

because it is full of ether. (Here the reason is ether, which has no locus).

A non-conclusive fallacy (*Anupasamhārī Hetvābhāsa*) has no either affirmative or negative examples. For example:

All things are impermanent,

because they are knowable.

The fallacious reason, which is the counterpart of that non-existent, which constantly accompanies the major term, is called contradictory fallacy *Viruddha Hetvābhāsa*. For example,

This hill is full of fire,

because it is full of water.

*Satpratipakṣa* fallacy seeks to establish the existence of probandum on one hand and provides the reason, which seeks to establish the non-existence of it. For example,

One reason - Sound is eternal, because it is audible.

Opposite reason - Sound is non-etelnal, because it is produced.

*Asiddha Hetvābhāsa* is of three kinds viz. *aśrayāsiddha, svarūpāsiddha and vyāpyatvāsiddha.* The fallacy, whose locus is not known, is called as *Āśrayāsiddha hetvābhāsa.* That is called *svarūpāsiddha Hetvābhāsa,* whose nature is not known to exist in the locus. And if the nature of a fallacious reason is not useful in establishing its invariable concomitance with the major term then that will be called as *vyāpyatvāsiddha hetvābhāsa,* which has been subdivided into three like: *sāsiddhi, hetvāsiddhi and vyāptyasiddhi.*

*Bādhita* fallacy occurs when the major term, which is assigned to minor term, does not exist in it. For example,

Fire is cold,

because it is a substance

*Gaṅgeśa* has divided it into ten such as *pakṣa pratyakṣa bādhita, pakṣa anumāna bādhita, pakṣa śabdabādhita* etc. *Viśwanātha* follows *Gaṅgeśa.* He changes *Bādhita* into *kālatyapadiṣta,* which has no further divisions. *Annaṃbhaṭṭ a* holds the views of *Gaṅgeśa.*

**The division:**

*Gaṅgeśa* has divided inference into three on the basis of the nature of *vyāpti,* such as *kevalānvayī, kevalavyatirekī and anvaya-vyatirekī*[32]. This classification of inference, in fact, is not new to the system. It has its origination in *Pariśuddhi,* the text of *Udayanācārya. Gaṅgeśa* does not follow the tradition of classifying inference into three such as *pūrvavat, śeṣavat and sāmānyatodṛṣṭa* (which is given by *Vātsyāyana). The kevalānvayī anumāna,* as *Gaṅgesa* defines, is an inference in which there is no negative example[33]. For example,

It is namable,

because it is knowable.

An exclusively negative inference or *kevalavyatirekī anumāna* has no affirmative example. Such as:

The Earth is different from the things, because it possesses smell.

The inference, which has both affirmative and negative examples, is called *anvaya-vyatirekī anumāna* . For example,

The hill has fire,

because it has smoke ( affirmative example)

as a kitchen and not as a lake (negative example)

We do not find such type of classification in *Viśwanātha's* text. According to *Annaṃbhaṭṭa,* above classification is exclusively meant for *hetu*[34].

**Another division**

We also find another type of division of inference such as: *svārtha* (inference for one's self) and *parārtha* (inference for others sake) the former is based on psychology whereas the later one is totally based on logic.

***Svārthānumāna***

A person, who repeatedly observes the togetherness (invariably connected) of smoke and fire in the kitchen etc., sees smoke from a distance. After seeing it he recollects that 'where there is smoke there is fire'. Then he realizes that the hill has smoke, which is invariably connected with fire. Finally, he reaches in the conclusion that the hill has fire. This process is called the process of inference for one's self.

***Parārthānumāna***

After inferring for himself same person proceeds to convince to others by employing five-membered syllogism. This is called an inference for the sake of others. The process goes on like this:

1. first of all he states that 'this hill has fire'—*Pratijñā*
2. because it has smoke—*Hetu*
3. where there is smoke there is fire like kitchen—*Udāharaṇa*
4. the smoke, possessed by the hill, is fire-pervaded—*Upanaya*
5. therefore, the hill has fire—*Nigamana*

The above five-membered syllogism generates the

inferential cognition of fire in other's mind. Hence it is called *parārthānumāna*. *Viśwanātha* remains silent on this point. *Annaṃbhaṭṭa* follows *Gaṅgeśa*[35].

**Members of syllogism:**

*Gaṅgeśa* strongly opposes to the definition of *avayavas* given by Old logicians[36]. *Avayavas,* according to him, is a sentence that gives rise to the knowledge, which contributes to the production of an entire knowledge, which produces consideration.[37] He also rejects the definition of *pratijñā* saying that 'the declaration of probandum cannot be a definition of *pratijñā,* because it suffers from over-application[38]. He defines *pratijñā* as 'is a sentence, which causes knowledge, whose object is the same as that of the conclusion and which contributes to the production of entire knowledge, which produces consideration[39]. *Gaṅgeśa* has prepared three alternative definitions of *hetu*[40]. All his definitions convey the meanings like '*hetu* produces the knowledge, that which gives rise to the consideration'. He has divided *hetu* into three classes like *anvayihetu, vyatirekihetu* and *anvayavyatirekihetu*[41].

There is no difference of opinion with old-logicians with regard to the definition of *udāharaṇa*. The only difference is its division. Old-logicians divides it under the name *sādharmya* and *vaidharmya,* whereas, *Gaṅgeśa* names it as *anvaya* and vyatireka[42]. *Gaṅgeśa* defines *Upanaya* as the cause of consideration and it is of two kinds such as *anvaya-upaṇaya* and *vyatireka-upanaya*[43]. *Nigamana* produces the klowledge of major term as indicated by that of middle term through its invariable concomitance. Hence, much difference is not seen on this point.

## FOOTNOTES

1. Opening statement of a booklet on "*Navya-nyāya* language and Methodology", published by SSUS, Kalady.

2. TSA—सर्वव्यवहारहेतुर्बुद्धिर्ज्ञानम्।
3. *Nyāyakośa,* p. 825 वुबोधयिषापूर्वकवाक्यप्रयोग: व्यवहार:।
4. TSA - सा (बुद्धि:) द्विविधा स्मृतिरनुभवश्च।
5. Ibid. - संस्कारमात्रजन्य ज्ञानं स्मृति:।
6. Ibid. - तदभाववति तदप्रकारको अनुभव: अयथार्थ।
7. TSA- परामर्शजन्य ज्ञानं अनुमिति।
8. Ibid. व्याप्तिविशिष्ट पक्षधर्मजाज्ञानं परामर्श:।
9. BP, verse- 66 व्यापारस्तु परामर्श:, करणं व्याप्तिधीर्भवेत्।
10. The fourth chapter carries the whole discussion.
11. *Liṅga* being known means it must be present at the time of inference.
12. BP, verse 67 ज्ञायमानं लिङ्गं तु करणं न हि।
13. तज्जन्यत्वे सति तज्जन्यजनको व्यापार:
14. NTK, p. 262
15. TCA व्याप्तिविशिष्ट पक्षधर्मताज्ञानजन्यं ज्ञानं अनुमिति:?
16. Ibid. तत्करणं अनुमानम्।
17. Ibid. तच्च लिङ्गपरामर्श:।
18. *TCA, anumiti prakaraṇa*....किन्तु व्याप्तिज्ञानं करणं परामर्शो व्यापर:।
19. BP, verse 66 व्यापारस्तु परामर्श: करणं व्याप्तिधी: भवेत्।
20. TCA-vyāptivāda नन्वनुमितिहेतुर्व्याप्तिज्ञाने का व्याप्ति:।
21. ICNN, p.126
22. TD, *anumānakhaṇḍa* धूमाग्नेयोर्व्याप्तिग्रहे साध्य-साधनयोर्भूय: साहचार दर्शनेन. .....
23. TCA, *parāmarśaprakaraṇa* व्याप्तिविशिष्ट पक्षधर्मताज्ञानं परामर्श:।
24. NSM, verse 68 वह्निव्याप्यधूमवानोऽयं पर्वत: इति ज्ञानं परामर्श:।
25. TSA लिङ्गपरामर्शोऽनुमानम्।
26. AP, p. 362
27. TCA, *Hetvābhāsaprakaraṇa* हेत्वाभासास्तत्त्वनिर्णय-विजयप्रयोजकत्वान्निरुप्यते।
28. Ibid. क. तत्रानुमितिकारणीभूताभावप्रतियोगियथार्थ ज्ञानविषयत्वम्।
    ख. यद्विषयकत्वेन लिङ्गज्ञानस्यानुमितिबन्धकत्वं तत्त्वम्।
    ग. ज्ञायमानं सदनुमितिप्रतिबन्धकं यत्तत्त्वं वा।
29. Ibid. ते च सव्यभिचारविरुद्धसत्प्रतिपक्षासिद्धबाधिता: पञ्च।
30. Ibid. साध्य संशयजनककोटिद्वियोपस्थापकपक्षधर्मताज्ञानविषयत्वे सति हेत्वभिमत: स: (सव्यभिचार:)

31. *The whole discussion on hetvābhāsa is based on hetvābhāsa-sāmānya-nirukti of Tatvacintāmaṇi*
32. TCA, *kevalānvayīprakaraṇa* तच्चानुमानं त्रिविधं केवलान्वयि-केवलव्यतिरेक्य-न्वयव्यतिरेकिभेदात्।
33. Ibid. असिद्धिपक्षं केवलान्वयी, तथाहि केवलान्वयिनोऽभिधेयस्य न विपक्षः।
34. TṢA—लिङ्गं त्रिविधं। अन्वयव्यतिरेकि केवलान्वयि केवलव्यतिरेकिचेति।
35. Vide TSA.
36. Ibid.
37. Ibid. अनुमितिचरमकारण-लिङ्ग-परामर्श प्रयोजक शब्दज्ञान-जनकवाक्यं न्यायः।
38. Ibid. तत्र न प्रतिज्ञा साध्य निर्देशः—साध्यपदेऽतिव्याप्तेः।
39. Ibid.
40. Ibid. क. हेतुत्वं च अनुमितिकारणीभुतलिङ्गपरामर्श प्रयोजक शब्दज्ञानजनक-साध्यविषयक शाब्दधीजनक हेतुविभक्ति मच्छब्दत्वम्।
    ख. प्रतिज्ञावाक्यधीजन्य कारणाकांक्षा विवर्तकज्ञानजनकहेतुमद्विभक्ति-मद्वाक्यत्वं वा।
    ग. हेतुत्वप्रतिपादक विभक्ति मन्यायावयवत्वं वा।
41. Ibid.
42. AP, p. 356
43. Ibid, p. 459

# CHAPTER VI
# CONCEPT OF TṚTĪYALIṄGAPARĀMARŚA AND ITS NECESSITY

**Though *parāmarśa* has different names still its nature and function is same**

*Naiyāyikas* have used the term *parāmarśa* with a nomenclature. In some texts it is used as *liṅgaparāmarśa*,[1] somewhere it is *tṛtīyaliṅgaparāmaśa*[2]. Somewhere it is *tṛtīyaliṅgadarśana*[3] whereas, somewhere it is only *parāmarśa*[4]. Though *parāmarśa* has been used in different names still its nature and function has been kept unchanged. It is called *liṅgaparāmarśa* because it is such a knowledge of probans, which establishes the inferring object through a relation called invariable concomitance[5]. This is called *tṛtīyaliṅgaparāmarśa* (third time perception of the probans) because it is the last of the cognition of smoke, which is essential for the inference of fire. Let us see how it happens. Someone, for the first time, perceives smoke invariably connected with fire in a place like kitchen etc. A frequent perception of such case generates knowledge in his mind like *"vahnivyāpya dhūma"* (smoke is pervaded by fire). That which covers a wider area is called *vyāpaka*. For example, fire. And that which covers a less area is called *vyāpya*. For example, smoke. So, fire is the pervader and smoke is the pervaded one. This can be presented in the following way:

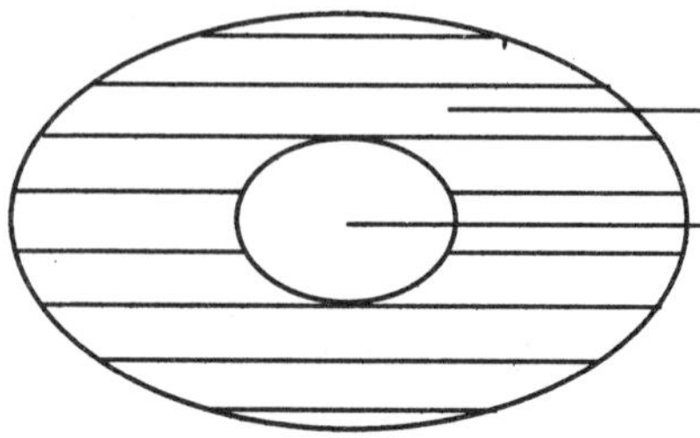


This knowledge of invariably connected fire and smoke in the kitchen etc. is called first perception of the probans or प्रथमलिङ्ग परामर्श. This knowledge leaves an impression like 'smoke is pervaded by fire'. After that another smoke happens to be seen by the same person somewhere in mountain etc. This is called the second perception of smoke or द्वितीयलिङ्ग परामर्श. Here the recollection of the impression, left by the first perception of the probans, will occur. Again this recollection does not produce the result i.e. inferential cognition immediately. There will be a further recollection of smoke. This smoke is not like an ordinary one. It is that smoke, which exists in the inferential subject, is invariably connected with fire. This is called third perception of the probans or तृतीयलिङ्ग परामर्श, which is known as an immediately preceding cause *(carama kāraṇa)* of inferential cognition. In short, the probans i.e. smoke is known for the first time when we observe its invariable relation with the probandum i.e. fire in the kitchen etc. It is known for second time when it is related to the inferential subject. It is considered for the third time when we know it as a property of the inferential subject, which is invariably related to the probandum. Immediately after that the inferential cognition arises[6]. It is also called *tṛtīyaliṅgadarśana*[7], because the *liṅga* or smoke is being perceived third time in the whole process. Finally, it is called *parāmarśa* or confirmatory cognition because it confirms that the probans, exists in the inferential subject, is qualified by invariable comsomitance

**Nature of parāmarśa: What is *parāmarśa?***

*Parāmarśa,* according to *Gaṅgeśa,* is the cause of *anumiti* i.e. inferential cognition. He defines it as the knowledge of the property of the subject, which is qualified by invariable concomitance[8]. This *parāmarśa* produces *anumiti.* In other words, *anumiti* is ultimately dependent on *parāmarśa,* which is again dependent on the probans. If it is a *sad-hetu,* it produces a valid *parāmarśa* and a valid *parāmarśa* generates a valid inference. *Mathurānātha Tarkavāgiśa,* a celebrated commentator of *Tatvacintāmaṇi,* clarifies *Gaṅgeśa's* statement. He holds *pakṣadharma* as *pakṣasambadha* and *vyāptivisiṣṭa* means *vyāptivisiṣṭe jñānaṃ (saptamī tatpuruṣa)* keeping its meaning unchanged[9]. The same idea reflects *Nyāyasiddhāntamuktāvalī. Viśvanātha* defines *parāmarśa* as the knowledge that the concomitant *(vyāpya)* exists in the subject *(pakṣa)*[10]. It means the knowledge, which confirms the relation of what is possessed of invariable concomitance is called *parāmarśa*[11]. Thus, *parāmarśa* has been defined by *Navya Naiyāyikas.*

**How does it occur?**

*Naiyāyikas* have followed a systematic process of inference in which *parāmarśa* is supposed to be a part. It is a part because it helps in forming the whole i.e. inference. Then the basic question arises like 'How does that occur, which helps something else in occuring?' *parāmarśa* is a combination of two knowledges. The first one is a recollection (of *vyāpti)* and the second one is an experience (of that recollection i.e. that *vyāptivisiṣṭa hetu* exists in the mountain) i.e. *hetu* is *vyāptivisiṣṭa.*

The process continues like this: first of all a person perceives an invariably connected smoke in the kitchen etc. From this perception he comes to know that 'smoke is pervaded by fire'. Then he proceeds towards mountain where he happens to see smoke from a distance *(hetudarśana)*. After seeing it he recollects the relationship of smoke and fire like 'where there is smoke there is fire' *(vyāptismaraṇa)*. After that he joins the previous knowledge *(dhūmavahni-vyāpya)* with the current one *(yatra dhūma tatra vahni)* and forms a third kind of knowledge i.e. the smoke, which exists in the mountain, is invariably connected by fire. This knowledge is known as *parāmarśa* or confnmatory cognition. In the very next moment the knowledge of fire i.e. 'mountain possesses fire' arises there. This is called *anumiti* and the component, which produces this knowledge, is called *parāmarśa*.

## Constituents of *parāmarśa*

*Parāmarśa* is *vyāptiviśiṣṭa-pakṣadharmatājñāna* i.e. the knowledge of *pakṣadharmatā,* which is *vyāptiviśiṣṭa*. This shows that *parāmarśa* has two components. The first component is *vyāptiviśiṣṭa,* it means 'that which is qualified *by vyāpti'*. Here, the word 'that' means 'something', which is characterized by *vyāpti*. The second component is *pakṣadharmatā*. It is defined as *"vyāpyasya hetoḥ pakṣa-vṛttitvaṃ"*[12] i.e. the existence of hetu on *pakṣa*. A question can be raised here like 'are all the objects, existing on mountain, called *pakṣadharma*?' The answer is obviously 'no'. Because though all smokes are pervaded by fire still we cannot say that all smokes are *paṣadharma* because there should be a desire to infer. So, a particular smoke, which is present in the inferential subject at the time of inference, will be called as *pakṣadharma* and *pakṣadharmatā* is the property, which exists in the *pakṣadharma*. These are two separate components. When they come together they constitute a whole and that is called *parāmarśa.* So, *parāmarśa* is a knowledge of the property of the mountain qualified by invariable concomitance.

**Function of *parāmarśa***

*Parāmarśa* functions as *vyāpāra* in the process of inference, because the inferential cognition takes place through it. There is a controversy regarding the function of *parāmarśa,* Old logicians hold it as an instrument, because it produces an immediate result whereas, new logicians oppose it. If it is a *karaṇa,* argue new logicians, then there will not arise inferential cogrātion from the smoke which was in the past time and which will be in the future time[13].

***Paramarśa is the vyāpāra* of the process of inference:**

We have discussed the definition of *karaṇa* and *vyāpāra* in the last chapter. Now we will see whether this *parāmarśa* acts as *karaṇa* or *vyāpāra* in the process of inference. In this connection *Gaṅgesa* opines thus: *parāmarśa* is not an instrument because it has absence of intermediate function[14]. He strongly holds *parāmarśa* as an ultimate reason *(carama kāraṇa)* of the process of inference[15]. The later logicians have accepted *Gaṅgeśa.* But it is *Annaṃbhaṭṭa,* who holds *parāmarśa* as an instmment of the process of inference[16].

**Its necessity:**

*Mīmāṃsakas* argue like 'why *anumiti* does not arise from the second perception of the probans (द्वितीयलिङ्ग परामर्श). Here also the doubt about the existence of fire is certainly there. What is the need of accepting a third time perception of the probans then?'[17]. "Yes you are right", reply *Naiyāyikas,* "you just imagine of a person who has not ascertained *vyāpti* or has forgotten it, will he be able to draw inference?" Therefore, the third time perception of probans is very much essential, because after observing smoke in the subject and after recollecting *vyāpti* a third cognition is necessary to cause the inferential cognition. This third cognition called *parāmarśa* or *liṅgaparāmarśa* or *tṛtīyaliṅgaparāmarśa*"[18].

In *Tarkadīpikā Annaṃbhaṭṭa* shows the necessity of accepting *tṛtīyaliṅgaparāmarśa* saying 'there is necessity of accepting *tṛtīyaliṅgaparāmarśa* otherwise the expression like 'hill has smoke, which is invariably connected by fire' cannot generate verbal understanding. Therefore, for the uniformity in logic the concept should be accepted.'[19]

## FOOTNOTES

1. NV 1.1.5 तदिदमन्तिमं प्रत्यक्षं पूर्वाभ्यां प्रत्यक्ष्याभ्यां स्मृत्या गृह्यमाणं परामर्शरूपमनुमानं भवति।
2. TCA. पक्षधर्मे व्याप्तिविशिष्टज्ञानं तदनन्तरं विशिष्टवैशिष्टयज्ञानं पक्षे वा तृतीयलिङ्ग-परामर्शः—तत्वचिन्तामणि, परामर्श प्रकरणम्।
3. व्याप्तिस्मृति............द्वितीयलिङ्गदर्शनादेवानुमिति......तृतीयलिङ्गदर्शनकल्पन-मिति।—न्यायपरिचय
4. व्यापारस्तु परामर्शः करणं व्याप्तिधीर्भवेत्—न्यायसिद्धान्तमुक्तावली
5. *Siddānta candrodaya a commentary on Tarkasaṃgraha by Śrikṛṣṇa Dhūrjaṭi as it is quoted in Athale and Bodas p.* 254 व्याप्तिवलेन लीनमर्थं गमयतीति लिङ्गं तच्च धूमादिस्तस्य परामर्शो ज्ञानविशेषः।
6. लिङ्गलिङ्गिसम्बन्धदर्शनमाद्यं प्रत्यक्षम्, लिङ्गदर्शनं द्वितीयम्। बुभुत्सावतो द्वितीयलिङ्ग-दर्शनात् संस्काराभिव्यत्क्युत्तरकालं स्मृतिः, स्मृत्यनन्तरं च पुनर्लिङ्गदर्शनमयं धूम इति।—न्यायवार्त्तिक १.१.५
7. प्याप्तिस्मृति........द्वितीयलिङ्गदर्शनादेवानुमिति....तृतीयलिङ्गदर्शनकल्पनमिति।—न्यायपरिचय
8. पक्षधर्मस्य व्याप्तिविशिष्टज्ञानमनुमितिहेतुः।—तत्वचिन्तामणि, परामर्श प्रकरणम्
9. पक्षधर्मस्य पक्षसम्बन्धस्य व्याप्तिविशिष्टज्ञानं व्याप्तिविशिष्टेज्ञानम्। मथुरानाथ
10. BP-68 व्याप्यस्य पक्षवृत्तित्वधीः परामर्श उच्यते।
11. NSM-68 व्याप्तिविशिष्टस्य पक्षेण सह वैशिष्ट्यावगाहिज्ञानम्।
12. *Bhāṣāpariccheda*-68
13. NSM-67 अत्र प्राचीनास्तु व्याप्यत्वेन ज्ञायमानं लिङ्गमनुमिति वदन्ति.....यद्यनुमितौ लिङ्गं करणं स्यात्तदानागतेन लिङ्गेन विनष्टेन लिङ्गेन चानुमितिर्न स्यादनुमिति करणस्य लिङ्गगस्य तदानीमभावादिति।

14. TCA, *parāmarśa prakaraṇam* यत्तु व्यापारभावान्न परामर्शः करणमेते तथैव, किन्तु व्याप्तिज्ञानं करणं परामर्शो व्यापारः।
15. Ibid. किञ्च लिङ्गकरणत्वपक्षे परामर्श एव तदव्यापारः परामर्शस्य तु न व्यापारमस्ति चरमकारणत्वादिति न तत्करणम्।
16. *Tarkasaṃgraha* स्वार्थानुमितिपरार्थानुमित्योर्लिङ्गपरामर्श एव करणम्।
17. अथ पर्वतगतमात्रस्य पुंसो यद्धूमज्ञान, तत् कथं नाग्निमनुमापयैत? अस्ति चात्राग्नि सन्देहः। साधकवाधकप्रमाणाभावेन संशयस्य न्यायप्राप्तत्वात्। Tarkabhāṣā anumānakhaṇḍa.
18. सत्यम्। अगृहितव्याप्तेरिव गृहित......तेन धूमदर्शने जाते व्याप्तिस्मृतौ भूतायां यद्धूमज्ञानं तत्तृतीयं 'धूमवाश्चाचम्' इति......स एव लिङ्गपरामर्शः। Ibid.
19. वह्निव्याप्यधूमवानमयमिति शाब्दपरामर्शस्थले परामर्शस्यावश्यकतया लाघवेन सर्वत्र परामर्शस्यैव कारणत्वात्। लिङ्ग न करणम् अतीतानागतादौ व्यभिचारात्। व्यापारवत्कारणं करणमिति मते परामर्शद्वारा व्याप्तिज्ञानं करणम्।

## CHAPTER VII

# OBJECTION RAISED AGAINST *TṚTIYALIṄGAPARĀMARŚA*

"Your conviction that the third perception is the ultimate cause of the inferential cognition is totally baseless." This is just a challenge of *Mīmāṃsakas* put to the *Nayiyāyikas*. The *Nayiyāyikas,* on the other hand, entertain such type of challeging discussions in an enthusiastic manner. It is *Raghunātha Śiromaṇi,* who invited others saying *"duṣyaṃ me vacaḥ paraṃ nipuṇaṃ vibhāvya"* (I welcome you to criticize me, but think hundred times before doing so). By tracing the history of *Nyāya-Vaiśeṣika* system of Indian intellectual tradition it can be observed that the entire *Nyāya* system has been developed in a dialogue form. Dialogue between two systems, viz. *Nyāya* and *Buddhist, Nyāya* and *Mīmāṃsā* etc.

In the same way, *Liṅgaparāmarśavāda,* a chapter of the text *Nyāyasiddhāntadvīpa* of *Śaśadhara,* is written in a dialogue form. Here, there is a controversy between *Nyāya* and *Mīmāṃsā* regarding *parāmarśa.*

Both the participants have strong arguments over the issue called *parāmarśa* like it should be regarded as a special component in the process of inference or not. But both have the agreement over the statement that the knowledge of the existence of the probans on the subject is the cause to the inferential cognition.

However, this chapter deals with the objections raised by the opponents. The entire dialogue has been quoted from the chapter called *Liṅgaparāmarśavāda* of *Śaśadhara*.

**Objection no. 1 :—**

Is it the case that a qualified cognition is the cause of an inferential cognition on account of positive or negative concomitance? Or, in some other way?

Here the author presents the position of *Mīmāṁsakas*. *Naiyāyikas* standpoint is that the qualified cognition is the cause of an inferential cognition. 'But in what form?' asks *Mīmāṁsaka*. Is that the cause of an inferential cognition on account of either positive or negative concomitance? Or in some other way? These are two alternatives left with *Naiyāyikas*. The first alternative can be explained in this way: positive concomitance means the presence of something is dependent upon the presence of another thing. For example,

+X = +Y (positive concomitance)

Negative concomitance means the absence of something occurs due to the absence of another thing. For example,

-X = -Y (negative concomitance)

Now, *Mīmāṃsakas* are asking to the *Naiyāyikas* that is it the case that the presence of that qualified knowledge causes the inference and its absence causes the absence of it? This can be presented in this way:

+qualified knowledge = +inference

-qualified knowledge = - inference

Or do you have any other way out to prove this?

**Objection no. 2 :—**

You are *(Naiyāyikas)* postulating the causal relationship between *parāmarśa* and *anumiti,* but it is not acceptable, because the force of the principle of elimination gets exhausted over there where we find a form 'the state of being a smoke' which is different from the form 'the state of being something'.

Again, it is not possible to postulate that the *parāmarśa* is the cause of inferential cognition, because when that *parāmarśa* itself is not there then how will it be the cause of *anumiti?*

Therefore, the *parāmarśa* , as postulated by you *(Naiyāyikas),* cannot be established.

**Objection no. 3 :—**

Well, if you claim saying that the eause of direct perception is stronger than the cause of inferential cognition then this is also not acceptable, because in that case it will lead to a continuous flow of the third perception and also because it will lead to contingency of awareness.

**Objection no. 4 :—**

Again, your saying that 'the powerfulness of the factors of an inferential cognition will lead to a continuous flow of inferential cognition and in that case, the knowledge that 'I am inferring' will not arise' is also not acceptable, because the earlier factors have already produced the result, so other factors will not arise since the result has not already come into existence.

Therefore, there is no possibility of the third perception due to the absence of the cause.

**Objection no. 5:—**

Again, if you say that 'well, that does not matter if *parāmarśa* is not possible there (i.e. *parāmarśa* is not the cause of inferential cognition) but let the senses be the cause there (i.e. in the process of interence)'. This is also not being accepted, because the absence of the contact with the object.

**Objection no. 6 :—**

Again, if you say that when the smoke is presented by another knowledge (i.e. remembrance) then there will arise a mental perception of *parāmarśa*. This is also not right, because mind has no capacity to cause a cognition of an external object.

**Objection no. 7 :—**

You cannot say that 'let us assume that the impression of that object will generate the mental perception of the *parāmarśa,* because impression of what? Since there was no experience of mountain possessing smoke, which is pervaded by fire.

**Objection no. 8 :—**

Again, how do you *Naiyāyikas* support third perception? Because it is not possible to know the state of being pervaded by the difference of other than the Earth in the probans, namely, the *Pṛithivitva.*

**Objection no. 9 :—**

Well, if you say that whatever is pervaded in reality, the knowledge of that qualified by 'some-thing-ness' is the cause of the inferential cognition then what type of inferential cognition is going to be established over there? The inferential cognition presented by a particular probans or a probans in general?

**Objection no. 10 :—**

Again, if you say that whatever is not pervaded by fire in reality such as a beam of the dust, even from the qualified knowledge of that, there arises the inferential cognition of fire. This is also not accepted, because I *(Mīmāṃsaka)* don't accept that such an inferential cognition arises there. Assuming your *(Naiyāyikas)* standpoint to be true if we analyze it then such an inferential cognition can be explained to have arisen from the cognition of that which is, in reality, pervaded by fire.

Therefore, your conviction that the third perception is the ultimate cause of inferential cognition is totally baseless.

Hence, there is no cause and effect relation between *parāmarśa* and *anumiti*

## CHAPTER VIII
# ŚAŚADHARA'S REPLY TO THE OBJECTIONS

This chapter presents the replies made by *Śaśadhara*

**Your (Mīmāṃsakas) objection :**

Is it the case that a qualified cognition is the cause of an inferential cognition on account of positive or negative concomitance? Or, in some other way?

**Our (Naiyāyikas) reply (no. 1) :—**

In that case the second alternative holds true. Because even if, after the remembrance of the invariable concomitance, there can not arise an inferential cognition though there arises a cognition of existence of the smoke 'in some form' in the subject. And this 'other fonn' is nothing but 'the state of being pervaded by the probandum by the thing of elimination'.

Thus, the qualified cognition i.e. *parāmarśa* gets established.

**Your objection :**

You are postulating that *parāmarśa* cannot be a causal factor to *anumiti,* because the force of the principal of elimination gets exhausted there where we find a form of 'the state of being smoke', which is different from the form 'the state of being something'.

Again, *parāmarśa* is not the cause, because when it *(parāmarśa* ) itself is not there how it will be the cause of *anumiti*.

**Our reply (no. 2) :—**

The process of inference has not been terminated there, because all the necessary factors have not been taken into consideration.

Again, to your second objection that *parāmarśa* itself is not there, we have this to say that *parāmarśa* is there but you are not accepting it, because you follow a mechanical process of inference whereas, we are interested in the epistemology of inferential cognition.

Hence, to generate a particular variety of *anumiti* we need a confirmatory perception.

Thus, the *parāmarśa* gets established.

**Your objection :**

Your conviction that the cause of direct perception is not stronger than the cause of inferential cognition, because it will lead to a continuous flow of the third perception and also it will lead to contingency of awareness.

**Our reply (no. 3) :—**

To answer this we say that there is no such chance of chain since after *parāmarśa* the *anumiti* will be produced and there will end one process. If someone wants to infer again then a fresh process will begin. Therefore, there is no chance of any continuity of *parāmarśa*.

**Your objection :**

You are not accepting that the powerfulness of the factors of an inferential cognition will lead to a continuous flow of inferential cognition and in that case the knowledge that 'I am inferring' will not arise. And in the reply you are telling that 'if you accept it then the result will not come into being, because the earlier factors have produced the result' .

**Our reply (no. 4) :—**

This is also not tenable, because once the *parāmarśa*-stage is reached it will definitely produce the result namely, the *anumiti*.

**Your objection :**

You are telling that senses cannot be the cause there, because of the absence of the contact with the object.

**Our reply (no. 5) :—**

This is absurd, because this is not the process of perception and hence we cannot expect the contact with object.

**Your objection :**

You are telling that when the smoke is presented by another knowledge (remembrance) then there will not arise a mental perception of *parāmarśa,* because mind has no capacity to cause a cognition of an internal object.

**Our reply (no. 6) :—**

This is also not tenable. Because mind is the common cause of any cognition and over and above this it can reveal external objects too. Moreover, *parāmarśa* is not a mental perception.

**Your objection :**

You are also telling that the impression of that object cannot generate the mental perception of *parāmarśa*, because there was no experience of mountain possessing smoke, which is pervaded by fire.

**Our reply (no. 7) :—**

This is also not reasonable because the inferential cognition of fire is not a remembrance.

**Your objection :**

Again, you are telling that the third perception should

not be entertained, because it is not possible to know the state of being pervaded by the difference of other than the Earth in the probans, namely, *Pṛthivitva.*

**Our reply (no. 8) :—**

This is not a case of *kevala-vyatireki-anumāna*. Therefore, your objection does not hold good here.

**Your objection :**

You don't accept that whatever is pervaded in reality, the knowledge of that qualified by 'some-thing-ness' is the cause of inferential cognition. And you want to know whether such inferential cognition is presented by a particular probans or a probans in general.

**Our reply (no. 9) :—**

The invariable concomitance is always between two universals and hence the objection, raised by you, holds no ground.

**Your objection :**

You don't accept that whatever is not pervaded by fire in reality such as a beam of dust, even from the qualified knowledge of that there arises the inferential cognition of fire.

**Our reply (no. 10):—**

A false cognition of *vyāpti* will result into false *anumiti*. This does not rule out the possibility of a true cognition of *vyāpti* resulting into a valid inferential cognition.

There in the process of a true *anumiti,* the knowledge of *parāmarśa* is absolutely essential.

Thus, there is a causal relationship between *parāmarśa* and *anumiti*.

# CONCLUSION

Form whatever we have discussed so far; the following conclusions can be drawn:

1) *Mīmāṃsā* system of Indian philosophy holds that from the knowledge of invariable concomitance *(vyāptijñāna)* and the knowledge of the existence of the *hetu* on the inferential subject *(pakṣadharmatājñāna)* the inferential cognition can arise. If it is asked that 'what is the cause of an inferential cognition?' they will answer that 'the knowledge of the probans, which is an attribute of the inferential subject, is the cause there'. So, in this analysis there is no scope of accepting a qualified cognition in between.

2) Secondly, for the inference of others' sake *(parārthānumāna)* they require only three steps starting from either *pratijñā* or *udāharaṇa*. According to them, *upanaya* cannot be a factor of generating inferential cognition in others.

If this is accepted then the following problem may arise.

1) If from *vyāptijñāna* and *pakṣadharmatājñāna* the inferential cognition arises then the following problem may occur. Suppose we will imagine of a person (say, X), who has the knowledge of *vyāpti* and another person (say, Y), who has no knowledge

of *vyāpti,* happens to see smoke in the mountain then in this case *anumiti* may arise in 'Y', which is illogical, But if we accept *parāmarśa* this problem won't arise, because *parāmarśa* is a combination of these two knowledges.

2) Secondly, unless it is confirmed that the mark or probans, which is invariably related to the probandum, exists on the subject, the conclusion namely, 'the subject possesses probandum' cannot be drawn.

3) Moreover, there will arise no verbal understanding from the sentence called *upanaya* if *parāmarśa* is not accepted as a step in the process of inferential cognition.

The form of Inference with only three members comes closer to the fonn of Inference of Western tradition. In Western tradition the form is as follows:

'p' implies 'q'
there is 'p'
∴ there is q

The first step may be compared with the concept of *vyāpti* in the Indian tradition, the second step may be compared with *dvitīya-liṅgadarśana* and the third step may be compared with *nigamana*.

The *Naiyāyikas* process of Inference is not a mechanical form. They are interested in the epistemology of an inferential cognition. Hence, it is necessary for them to postulate a state of *parāmarśa* or a confirmatory perception or cognition to account for the entire process of generating a particular variety of cognition called *anumiti*. Therefore, in the *Nyāya-Vaiśeṣika* form of Inference the fourth *avayava* or sentence is absolutely necessary.

# PART - II

## Sanskrit Text of *Liṅgaparāmarśavāda* with English translation

# लिङ्गपरामर्शवादः
# Liṅgaparāmarśavādaḥ

**Introduction**

Till recently it was the common belief that *Gaṅgeśa* was the first logician to introduce *Navya-nyāya.* But after the publication of *Nyāyasiddhāntadīpa* of *Śaśadhara,* it is gradually becoming clear that *Navya-nyāya* did not start ftom *Gaṅgeśa;* but it started developing long before *Gaṅgeśa.* Because the genus of *Navya-nyāya* thought can be detected in the last phase of the development of *Prācīna-nyāya,* particularly in the works of *Udayanācārya. Śaśadhara's Nyāyasiddhānta-dīpa* reflects in a quite developed stage of *Navya-Nyāya. It* contains twenty-six issues relating to the *Navya-nyāya* system of philosophy and logic. One such discussion has been covered in the chapter called *Tṛtīyaliṅgaparāmarśa,* which is a component of the process of inferential cognition.

**Contains of the Text**

The *Mīmāṁsā* system of Indian philosophy holds a different view with regard to the process of inferential cognition. They do not accept the component called *Tṛtīyaliṅgaparāmarśa. Śaśadhara* presents this dialogue between the *Mimāṁsākas* and the *Navya Naiyāyikas.* In *liṅgaparāmarśavāda,* which forms a chapter of his *Nyāyasiddhāntadīpa,* he presents all views on this issue available at his time and examines them one by one and presents the view of *Navya Naiyāyikas* in the conclusion.

*Nyāyasiddhāntadīpa* starts from *maṅgalavāda* and ends with *abhāvavāda*. The specialty of this text is that it takes up the views of the opponents, analyzes it thoroughly, refutes it one by one and finally gives his own opinion.

**Commentators of *Nyāyasiddhāntadīpa***

Among the commentaries available on *Nyāyasiddhānta-dīpa* the commentary of *Guṇaratna sūri* comes first. But it is a matter of controversy that four persons are being identified by the same name[1]. However, the person, who flourished in between 1400 to 1450 AD, is supposed to be the commentator of NSD[2]. Unfortunately we find commentary of *Guṇaratna sūri* only on four chapters of NSD. Rest are either lost or have not been commentated upon. Apart from this, we have another commentator on NSD called *Nyāyasiddhāntadīpaṭikā* by *Śeṣānanta*.

On the other hand, the date of *Śaśadhara* is also a controversial issue. However, he is supposed to have flourished in 12th century[3].

**1. Ipv[4] text:** इहानुमितौ लिङ्गस्य पक्षधर्मताप्रकारकं ज्ञानं कारणमित्युभयवादिसिद्धम्।

**Translation:** Both the participants (i.e. the *Naiyāyikas* and the *Mīmāṁsakas)* in the debate agree with the statement that with reference to the effect namely, an inferential cognition, the knowledge of the existence of the probans on the subject is the cause.

**2. lpv text:** तस्य ज्ञानस्य व्याप्तिप्रकारकत्वेनानुमितिकारणत्वं न वा, व्याप्तिविशिष्टपक्षधर्मताविशिष्टज्ञानमनुमितिकारणं न वेति विप्रतिपत्तिसङ्क्षेपः।

**Translation:** (However, there is a disagreement with regard to the fact) Whether such a cognition of the probans is the cause of the inferential cognition either in the form of a cognition, in which an invariable concomitance appears as a qualifier or not. Or whether such a cognition in the form of a knowledge which is qualified by the state of being located in the subject and which is qualified by the invariable concomitance or not. This, in short, is the bone of contention.

**3. lpv text:** तत्र परेषामयमाशयः। विशिष्टज्ञानस्य किमन्वयव्यतिरेकाभ्यामनुमितिकारणत्वमन्यथा वा।

**Translation:** Here what they mean is the following: *(Mīmāṃsakas position:)*

Is it the case that a qualified cognition is the cause of an inferential cognition on account of positive or negative concomitance? Or in some other way?

**4. lpv text**: न तावदाद्यः। अनुमितिपूर्वसमये व्याप्तिज्ञानपक्षधर्मताज्ञानव्यतिरिक्तस्य विशिष्टज्ञानस्यैवासिद्धेः।

**Translation:** The first alternative is not tenable. Because such a qualified cognition, other than the knowledge of invariable concomitance and the knowledge of the locatedness in the subject, cannet come into being before the coming into being of the inferential cognition.

**5. lpv text:** नन्वस्तु द्वितीयः। तथहि—व्याप्तिस्मरणान्तरं किञ्चित्वादिना रूपान्तरेण पक्षधर्मधूमज्ञानं कारणं वक्तव्यं,

**Translation:** *(Naiyāyikas intervention)* : Well, in that case let the second alternative hold true. It can be explained as follows :

There cannot arise an inferential cognition of fire even if there arises a cognition of the existence of the smoke 'in some form' in the subject after the remembrance of the invariable concomitance. Therefore, it is necessary to accept that the cognition of the smoke on the subject must be cause in 'some other form' before the arising of the inferential cognition.

**6. lpv text:** तच्च प्रकारान्तरं पारिशेष्याद् व्याप्यत्वमेवेति सिद्धं विशिष्टज्ञानमिति चेत्,

**Translation:** And 'other form' is nothing but 'the state of being pervaded by the probandum by the theory of elimination, and thus the qualified cognition (i.e. the *parāmarśa)* gets established.

**7. lpv text:** न, किञ्चित्वादिव्यतिरिक्तस्य धूमत्वादेरेव सम्भवे पारिशेष्यस्योपक्षीणत्वात्।

**Translation:** *(reply)* : It is not proper. Because when we can find another form 'the state of being a smoke' which is different from the form 'the state of having something', the force of the principle of the elimination gets exhausted.

**8. lpv text:** तथाहि–प्रथमं व्याप्तेः स्मरणमनुभवो वा अनन्तरं व्याप्यत्वावच्छेदकधूमत्वादि धर्मप्रकारकपक्षनिष्ठधूमज्ञानम्।

Translation: It can be explained as follows:—first of all there will arise the remembrance or experience of invariable concomitance and thereafter will arise the cognition of smoke, which is located in the subject, in which there is a property called 'smokeness', which is delimitor of the state of being pervaded (by the probamdum) appears as the qualifier.

**9. lpv text:** अनन्तरमव्यवहितसमय एवानुमितिरप्रत्यूहमुत्पद्यत एवेति। एवमप्युपपत्तौ अन्तरा विशिष्टज्ञानकल्पने तत्कारणत्वे च गौरवमेव बाधकम्।

**Translation:** Immediately after that the inferential cognition arises without any hindrance. When this can be explained in the above manner, it is cumbrousome to postulate a qualified cognition (i.e. *parāmarśa)* in the middle.

**10. lpv text:** न च विशिष्टज्ञानसामग्रीबलात् तत्कल्पनं युक्तं, कार्यासिद्धौ साम्ग्र्या अप्यसिद्धेः। सिद्धौ वाऽनुमितिसाम्ग्र्या बाधितत्वात्।

**Translation:** *(Mīmāṃsakas refute to the arguments of Naiyāyikas)*

It is not right to postulate that *(parāmarśa)* on the ground of the components of the qualified cognition (i.e. *parāmarśa),* because when the effect itself is not there how the components can be there? Granting that they are. there, it will be contradicted by the cause of inferential cognition.

**11. lpv text:** न चानुमितिसामग्र्यपेक्षया प्रत्यक्षसामग्री बलवतीति वाच्यम्। तृतीयलिङ्गपरामर्शधारावहनप्रसङ्गात्, तदनुव्यवसायप्रसङ्गाच्च।

**Translation:** It cannot be argued that the cause of direct perception is stronger than the cause of the inferential cognition. Because in that case it will lead to a continuous flow of the third perception, and also because it will lead to the contingency of awareness.

**12. lpv text:** न चानुमितिसामग्र्या बलवत्त्वेनानुमितिधारावहन-प्रसङ्गेनानुमिनोमीत्यनुव्यवसायो न स्यादिति वाच्यं, पूर्वसामग्र्या दत्तफलत्वाद-परसामग्रयाः सिद्धसाधनेनानुदयात्।

**Translation:** It cannot be said that due to the powerfulness of the factors of an inferential cognition it will lead to a continuous flow of inferential cognition, and in that case the knowledge that 'I am inferring' will not arise. Because the earlier factors have already yielded result, so other factors will not arise since the result has already come into being.

**13. lpv text:** अत एव धूमविशिष्टं पर्वतमुपलभ्य समयान्तरेऽपि व्याप्तिं स्मरतो वह्न्यनुमितिरुत्पद्यते।

**Translation**: This is why; there arises the inferential cognition of fire after perceiving the mountain, which is possessed of smoke even at later time for one who remembers the invariable concomitance.

**14. lpv text:** न हि तत्र तृतीयलिङ्गपरामर्शसम्भावनाऽपि कारणाभावात्। न हि तत्रेन्द्रियं कारणमसन्निकर्षात्।

**Translation:** There is no possibility of the third perception due to the absence of the cause. Sense organs cannot be the cause there,. because of the absence of the contact.

**15. lpv text:** न च ज्ञानान्तरोपनीते धूमे मानस एव परामर्श इति वाच्यम्। बहिर्विशेष्यके ज्ञाने मनसः सर्वथाऽसामर्थ्यात्। नापि संस्कारः पूर्व वह्निव्याप्यधूमवत्त्वेनाऽननुभवात्।

**Translation:** It cannot be said that when the smoke is presented by another knowledge (i.e. remembrance), there will arise a mental perception of *parāmarśa.* because mind has no capacity to cause a cognition of an external object. Even the impression cannot do it, because there was no experience of mountain possessing smoke, which is pervaded by fire.

**16. lpv text:** नाप्यानुमानिक एव परामर्शोऽनवस्थापात्।

**Translation:** One cannot say, either, that the cognition of *parāmarśa* is an inferential cognition here, because that will lead to the fault of endless regression.

**17. lpv text:** किञ्च केवलव्यतिरेक्यानुमानवादिना भवता कथं तत्र तृतीयलिङ्गपरामर्शः समर्थनीयः।

**Translation:** *(Mīmāṁsakas'* objection) : Moreover, how can you, who believe in *kevalavyatirekī-anumāna,* support third perception?

**18. lpv text:** इतरभेदव्याप्यत्वस्य पृथिवीत्वेऽग्रहात्, ग्रहे वा साध्यहेतु-नियतसामानाधिकरणस्य पृथिव्यां व्याप्तिग्राहकेणैव परिच्छिन्नत्वात् किमधिक-मनुमेयं स्यात्।

**Translation:** Because it is not possible to know the state of being pervaded by the difference of difference of other than the Earth in the probans namely, the *pṛthivītva.* Granting that you can know, what more is left to be inferred when the regular co-location of the probans and the probandum is already known in the Earth by the knowledge of invariable concomitance?

**19. lpv text:** व्यतिरेकव्याप्तिग्रहेणैव त्वद्दर्शने इतरभेदानुमितेः स्वीकृतत्वाच्च।

**Translation:** Also because in your theory it is accepted that the difference of difference other than (the Earth) is inferred by the knowledge of negative invariable concomitance.

**20. lpv text:** ननु तृतीयलिङ्गपरामर्शस्वीकुर्वता त्वया अनुमितित्वावच्छिन्नं कार्यं प्रति किमनुगतं कारणं वाच्यम्, न तावद्धूमवत्त्वादिविशिष्टपक्षपरामर्शोऽननुगमात्।

**Translation:** *(Naiyāyikas'* objection) : Well, what is the constant cause of the effect namely, any inferential cognition possessed of the state of the inferential cognition for you, who do not accept the third perception? You cannot reply by saying that the cognition, which reflects the subject possessing smoke, is the cause; because it cannot be a single uniform cause.

**21. lpv text:** नापि व्याप्यत्त्वावच्छेदकप्रकारकतद्विशिष्टपरामर्शः, उपजीव्यत्वेन व्याप्यत्वस्यैव तथात्वेनाङ्गीकारार्हत्वादिति।

**Translation:** Neither can you say that the qualified cognition, which reflects the probans, which possesses the state of being delimitor of pervaded-ness can be the cause; because the state of being pervaded alone is fit to be accepted as the cause.

**22. lpv text:** मैवम्। अनुमितित्वावच्छिन्नं प्रति व्याप्तिज्ञानस्यैव कारणत्वात्।

**Translation:** *(Mīmāṁsakas'* Reply) : It is not so, because the knowledge of invariable concomitance is the cause of any inferential cognition.

**23. lpv text:** धूमादिविशिष्टपक्षज्ञानस्य अनुमितिविशेष एवं प्रयोजकत्वात्। यद्वा यद् वस्तुगत्या व्याप्यं तद्विशिष्टज्ञानस्यैवानुमितिमात्रं प्रति प्रयोजकत्वात्।

**Translation:** The knowledge of the subject qualified by smoke is the cause of a particular inferential cognition. Or, whatever is pervaded in reality, the knowledge of 'something' qualified by that alone is the cause of any inferential cognition.

**24. lpv text:** न च यद्वस्तुगत्या व्याप्यं तस्य किञ्चित्त्वादिना रूपेण ज्ञानादनुमितिः स्यादिति वाच्यम्।

**Translation:** *(Mīmāṁsakas'* objection) : It cannot be said that whatever is pervaded in reality, the knowledge of that qualified by 'some-thing-ness' is the cause of the inferential cognition.

**25. lpv text:** तथाहि–किंरूपानुमितिस्तत्रापाद्यते। किं धूमादिलिङ्ग-विशेषोपहिता लिङ्गसामान्योपहिता वा।

**Translation:** It can be explained as follows:

What kind of inferential cognition is being established there? Is that inferential cognition presented by the particular probans namely smoke etc. or presented by probans in general?

**26. lpv text**: नाद्यः। धूमत्वादिप्रकारकज्ञानादेव तदुपपत्तेः।

Translation: The first alternative is not true. Because, it is possible to explain the arising of inferential cognition only from a cognition, which reflects smokeness as a qualifier.

**27. lpv text:** न द्वितीयः। तथाभूताया अनुमितेरेवासिद्धेः।

**Translation:** The second alternative is also not tenable. Because no such inferential cognition is known to exist.

**28. lpv text:** किञ्च यद्व्यतिरेकात् तृतीयलिङ्गपरामर्शः तत्र नोत्पद्यते तद्व्यतिरेकादेवानुमितिव्यतिरेकोपपत्तेः।

**Translation:** Moreover, it is possible to explain that without which (cause), the third perception does not arise from the absence of that alone, the inferential cognition will not arise.

**29. lpv text:** नन्वनुपपन्नमेतत्। यद्वस्तुगत्या वह्निव्याप्यं तद्विशिष्टज्ञानात् अनुमितिर्भविष्यतीति।

**Translation:** *(Naiyayika's* objection) : Well, this is not correct in reality to say that whatever is pervaded by fire from the knowledge of that the inferential cognition will arise.

**30. lpv text:** तथाहि—यद्वस्तुगत्या वह्निव्याप्यं नास्ति धूलिपटलादिकं तद्विशिष्टज्ञानादप्यनुमितिदर्शनादिति।

**Translation:** To elaborate: whatever is not pervaded by fire in reality such as: a beam of the dust, even from the qualified knowledge of that, there arises the inferential cognition of fire.

**31. lpv text:** मैवम्। मया तत्रानुमितेरेवाङ्गीकारात्। अङ्गीकारे वा यद्वस्तुगत्या वह्निव्याप्यं तद्भानादेवानुमित्युत्पत्तेः।

**Translation:** *(Mīmāṁsaka*'s reply:) It is not so, I don't accept that such an inferential cognition arises there. Granting it arises, it can be explained as follows: such an irferential cognition can be explained to have arisen from the cognition of that which is in reality pervaded by fire

**32. lpv text:** तस्मात् सर्वथानुपपन्नो लिङ्गपरामर्शस्य चरमकारणताभिमानो नैयायिकानामिति।

**Translation:** Your conviction that the third perception is the ultimate cause of the inferential cognition is totally baseless.

**33. lpv text:** प्राप्तेऽभिधीयते। व्याप्तिस्मरणानन्तरं किञ्चित्त्वादिना रूपेण धूमविशिष्टपर्वतज्ञानात् वह्निर्नानुमीयत इत्यविवादम्।

**Translation:** When such is the stand of the o' ponents we have the following to say: After remembering the invariable concomitance the knowledge of fire will not arise from the knowledge of mountain possessed of smoke in 'some form'; there is no dispute on this point.

**34. lpv text:** तत्र किं धूमत्वप्रकारकत्वव्यतिरेकाद् वा कार्यव्यतिरेकः कल्प्यताम्, तदव्याप्यत्वप्रकारकत्वव्यतिरेकाद्वा।

**Translation:** In such case, is it necessary to postulate that the absence of the effect depends on the absence of the knowledge of the smoke in which smokeness appears as a qualifier? Or, does it follow from the absence of the knowledge of that, in which 'the state of being pervaded by that (probandum)', appears as a qualifier?

**35. lpv text:** तत्र प्रथमस्य गौरवकरत्वात्, द्वितीयस्य व्याप्तिज्ञाने स्वीकारात् लघुत्वाच्च द्वितीय एव ज्यायान् एतदेवानुसन्धायाचार्यैरिदमुक्तम्–

"तत्र लिङ्गत्वोल्लेखि तृतीयं ज्ञानमेपितव्यम्" इति।

**Translation:** The first alternative is cumbersome. Since the second alternative is accepted in the knowledge of the invariable concomitance, and also because it is simpler, so the second one is more approaching.

Having kept this in mind *Udayanācārya* has said the following:

"In that case, it is necessary to accept the third perception."

**36. lpv text:** न च धूमाद्युपहितानुमितौ धूमत्वादिप्रकारकज्ञानस्य पूर्वमुपजीव्यत्वेन धूमत्वादिप्रकारककल्पनैव युक्तेति वक्तव्यम्।

**Translation:** You *(Mīmāṁsaka* ) cannot say that it is right to acccpt that—

Since with reference to the inferential cognition presented by the smoke, the knowledge in which smokeness appears, as a qualifier is the prior cause, it is proper to postulate the knowledge in which smokeness etc. is the qualifier (as the cause of the *anumiti).*

**37. lpv text:** तस्य हि अनुमितिविशेषं प्रति प्रयोजकत्वं न तु सामान्यं प्रति।

**Translation:** Because that is the cause of a particular inferential cognition and not of inferential cognition in general.

**38. lpv text:** प्रकृतेऽनुमितिमात्रं प्रति कारणतावच्छेदक: प्रकारो विचार्यते।

**Translation:** In the present context, we are discussing (what could be) the delimitor qualifier of the state of being the cause (of an inferential cognition in general).

**39. lpv text:** न च तथा धूमत्वादि। व्यभिचारात्।

**Translation:** Such as a qualifier cannot be 'smokeness', because it will lead to the violation of the cause-and-effect relationship.

**40. lpv text:** किंच तत्तदुपहितवह्न्यनुमितित्वं न धूमत्वादिप्रकारक-ज्ञानप्रयोज्यम्। किन्तु तत्तद्व्याप्यत्वप्रकारकज्ञानप्रयोज्यमेव।

**Translation:** Moreover, the inferential cognition of fire presented by a specific probans is not caused by the knowledge where smokeness is a qualifier, but is indeed caused by the knowledge where the state cf being pervaded by the probandum is the qualifier.

**41. lpv text:** धूमत्वादिप्रकारकज्ञानप्रयोज्यं तु धूमत्वादिविशिष्ट-ज्ञानत्वमेव। यत् पुनर्विकल्प्यापादनदूषणं कृतं तदापादनमात्रोच्छेदकत्वादुपेक्ष-णीयम्।

**Translation:** What is caused by the knowledge where smoke etc. are qualifier is the qualified knowledge of smoke, which possesses smokeness. The criticism, which was done postulating alternatives, needs to be ignored because of the destruction on the basis of those postulations.

**42. lpv text:** तथाहि–सामान्यप्रसिद्धिमादाय आपादनं प्रवर्त्तते न विशिष्यप्रसिद्धिं, तथैव सर्वत्र दर्शनात्।

**Translation:** It can be explained as follows:

Those alternatives are known by general knowledge but not by the knowledge in particular; this is how it is experienced everywhere.

**43. lpv text:** यत् पुनरुक्तं ज्ञानद्वयानन्तरं तृतीयं ज्ञानमुत्पद्यत इत्यसिद्धम्, अनुमितिसामग्रया: प्रतिबन्धकत्वादिति, तदपि मन्दम्।

**Translation:** Again, your saying that after those two knowledges there arises the third knowledge is not established, because the factors, which produce the knowledge of inferential cognition will become obstructing factors, is not sound.

**44. lpv text:** उक्तन्यायेन तत्कारणत्वव्यवस्थितौ तद्विरहेऽनुमिति-साम्ग्या: एवासिद्धे:।

**Translation.:** On the basis of the said logic when the causality of that (inferential cognition) is settled, in the absence of that cause, the factors of inferential cognition themselves are not established.

**45. lpv text:** केचित्तु ज्ञानद्वयानन्तरमेव तृतीयं विशिष्टज्ञानमुत्पद्यत इति न ब्रूम:, किन्तु व्याप्तिरूपविशेषणज्ञानसम्भवात् तद् द्वितीयज्ञानावसर एव वह्निव्याप्यधूमवानयमिति ज्ञानस्य सम्भवादित्यप्याहु:।

**Translation:** Some logicians argue as follows:

"We do not say that a third qualified knowledge arises after two knowledges, but what we say is when the knowledge of the qualifier namely, the invariable concomitance is possible. And it is also possible to have the qualified knowledge such as 'this (mountain) possesses smoke which is; pervaded by fire', at the moment of the second knowledge itself.

**46. lpv text:** न च व्याप्यत्वाज्ञानेऽपि धूमत्वाद्यवच्छेदकग्रहस्योपजी-व्यत्वात् स एवानुमितौ कारणमस्तु इति वाच्यम्।

**Translation:** It cannot be said that even in the absence of the knowledge of the 'state of being pervaded', since the knowledge of the delimitor such as smokeness etc. is the cause to the inferential cognition, let that alone be the cause of the inferential cognition.

**47. lpv text:** अवच्छेदकज्ञानं हि व्याप्यत्वसाक्षात्कारे कारणं, न तु व्याप्यत्वज्ञानमात्रे अवच्छेदकग्रहं विनापि वह्निव्याप्यावानयमिति वाक्याद् व्याप्यत्वज्ञानदर्शनात्।

**Translation:** Because the knowledge of the delimitor is the cause to the perception of the 'state of being pervaded', but not to any knowledge of 'the state of being pervaded'. Because in the absence of the knowledge of the delimitor, from the sentence that 'this (mountain) possesses smoke which is pervaded by the fire', the knowledge of 'the state of being pervaded' can arise.

**48. lpv text:** किञ्चैवमवच्छेदकज्ञानस्यापि कारणता न स्यात्, तत्रापि यदुपजीव्यं तदेव कारणमास्तामित्यस्यापि सुवचत्वात्।

**Translation:** Moreover, in this way, even the knowledge of the delimitor will not be the cause, because in such case, one can easily argue that whatever is the cause of that knowledge let that alone be the cause.

**49. lpv text:** एतेन व्याप्तिस्मरणेऽपि किञ्चित्त्वेन रूपेण पक्षधर्मधूमग्रहे सति यद्व्यतिरेकेण तृतीयलिङ्गपरामर्शव्यतिरेकः तद्व्यतिरेकेण ममाप्यनुमिति-व्यतिरेक इति निरस्तम्।

**Translation:** By this argument, even after the remembrance of invariable concomitance, if someone cognizes smoke existing on the subject in 'some form', even then, on the absence of whatever (say, 'x') there will be the absence of the third confirmatory perception. Due to the absence of that 'x', there will not arise any inferential cognition for me also. This argument is also turned down on the basis of this view.

**50. lpv text:** यदुक्तं-असन्निकृष्टे धूमे विशिष्टज्ञानासम्भव इति तदपि मन्दम्।

**Translation:** You said that 'the qualified knowledge is not possible there, because there is no contact with smoke'. It is not also a sound argument.

**51. lpv text:** तथाहि–परेणाऽपि तत्र व्याप्तिविशिष्टपक्षधर्मताज्ञान-मुत्पद्यते इति स्वीकर्त्तव्यम्। अन्यथा स धूमो वह्निव्याप्य इति व्यवहारो न स्यादिति।

**Translation:** It can be explained as follows:

Even the *Mīmāṁsaka* should accept that there (in the inferential cognition), the knowledge of the subject as having something qualified by the invariable concomitance arises. Otherwise, there will not be a linguistic expression as that 'smoke is pervaded by the fire'.

**52. lpv text:** तस्मादुभयवादिसमाधेयमेतत् किं निष्टङ्कनेन।

**Translation:** Therefore, why do you unnecessarily raise the argument when both the participants are to address the same question?

**53. lpv text**: तथापि–सुहृद्भावेन किं तत्र कारणमिति ब्रूषे तदा शृणु-ज्ञानान्तरोपनीते धूमे संयुक्तसमवेतलक्षणया प्रत्यासत्त्या ज्ञानरूपया मन एव तत्र कारणम्।

**Translation:** Still, if you are asking in a friendly manner 'what is the cause there?' then listen:—Mind is the only cause there through the relationship of remembrance of smoke, which will arise through the relationship of inherence with what is connected with it.

**54. lpv text:** न च वहिर्विशेष्यके प्रत्यये मनसो न स्वातन्त्र्यमति-प्रसङ्गादिति वाच्यम्। ज्ञानान्तरोपनयस्यैव नियामकत्वात्।

**Translation:** You should not argue by saying that mind cannot be a cause with regard to a cognition of an external object (smoke), because it does not have such freedom. (Because) that will lead to a fault called over-application. Because, the presentation of another type of cognition (by mind), will be a controlling factor there.

**55. lpv text:** न च विशेषणतया प्रत्यासत्या विशेषणमेव भासते इति वाच्यम्।

**Translation:** You cannot say that 'by the relationship of qualifierness, a qualifier alone can appear.

**lpv text:** इह भूतले घटाभाव इत्यत्राभावविशेष्यकस्य प्रत्ययस्य दर्शनात्। जम्बीरस्य रूपरसाविति सर्वसाधारणप्रत्ययाच्च।

**Translation:** Because in the expression 'there is absence of a pot on this ground', one can see the knowledge in which the absence of the pot *(ghaṭābhāva)* appears as a qualificand. It is also a common knowledge that in the knowledge 'the color and taste of a blackberry', the 'color and taste' appear as a qualificand.

**56. lpv text:** न चैवमनुमित्युच्छेदः सर्वत्र ज्ञानान्तरोपनीतस्य वह्नेर्भानसम्भवादिति वाच्यम्।

**Translation:** You cannot say that in this way no category of an inferential cognition will be left, because of the possibility of appearing of fire presented by the remembrance in all cases.

**57. lpv text:** न हि ज्ञानान्तरोपनीते भानेऽनुमितिव्यवहारोऽतिप्रसङ्गात्।

**Translation:** There is no experience of calling the knowledge presented by the remembrance as an inferential cognition, because of over-application.

**58. lpv text:** न हि मनोजन्यतामात्रेण मानसत्वं किन्तु असाधारणकारणान्तरनिरपेक्षमनोजन्यत्वेन।

**Translation:** Simply because a cognition is caused by mind it is not called 'mental perception', but it is called so only when it is caused by mind not depending on any other factor. But this is not the case with regard to an inferential cognition, etc.

**59. lpv text:** न चानुमित्यादौ तथा। परामर्शादिरसाधारणस्य कारणस्यापेक्षानियमात्।

**Translation:** (Because) there (in the inferential cognition), there is an invariable necessity of a special cause like *parāmarśa* etc.

**60. lpv text:** यद्वाऽनुमानादेव तत्र परामर्श उत्पद्यते, न चानवस्थादोषः, क्वचित् स्मृतावेव विश्रान्तेः।

**Translation:** Or, (let us accept) from the process of *anumiti* i.e. from *anumāna* alonc the knowledge of confirmatory cognition *(parāmarśa)* arises. It will not lead to the fault of endless regression, because of the termination of the process after remembrance (of the probandum) somewhere.

**61. lpv text:** अन्ये नु परामर्शे पक्षविशेष्यकत्वमतन्त्रमेव। किन्तु पक्षवृत्तेर्विशेष्यस्य व्याप्यत्वं गृह्यते यत्र तत्रानुमितिरुत्पद्यते।

**Translation:** Some logicians hold that in a confirmatory knowledge the adjunct 'the subject is a qualificand' is not important. But what is important is 'where the property of the subject (namely smoke) is known as pervaded (by fire), there arises the inferential cognition.

**62. lpv text:** एवम्भूतश्च तत्र परामर्शः, पक्षवृत्तिर्वह्निव्याप्य इति। अयमप्यनुमितिरूप एव।

**Translation:** Thus, the form of the confirmatory knowledge there will be 'whatever exists on the subject (i.e. the property of the subject) is pervaded by fire'.

This cognition also is the form of an inferential cognition only.

**63. lpv text:** अत्र धूमत्वमेव लिङ्गं धूमत्वस्य वह्निव्याप्यत्वं व्यक्त्यन्तरसन्निकर्षात् गृह्यते। असन्निकृष्टपर्वतवृत्तिधूमसम्बन्धितापि प्रत्यक्षेणैव गृह्यते।

Here, smokeness is the probans and that smokeness is known as pervaded by fire from the contact of another individual smoke. The relatedness of the smoke existing on the mountain, which is beyond the range of contact with eyes, is also known by perception alone.

64. lpv text: तस्मात् प्रत्यक्षरूपादेव परामर्शात्पर्वतवृत्तिः स धूमो वह्निव्याप्य इति अनुमितिरूपः परामर्शो जायते। तस्मात् परामर्शात् पर्वतो वह्निमानित्यनुमितिरुत्पद्यते इति न किञ्चिदनुपपन्नमित्याहुः।

**Translation:** Therefore, from the perceptual confirmatory cognition an inferential confirmatory cognition, which is of the form of 'that smoke existing on the mountain is pervaded by fire'. From that confirmatory cognition the inferential cognition namely 'the mountain has fire' arises. And hence, there is nothing inexplicable.

**65. lpv text:** यत्तु केवलव्यतिरेकानुपपत्तिरुक्ता तदपि मन्दम्।

**Translation:** Your other argument of impossibility of applying *kevalavyatireki-anumāna* is also not sound.

**66. lpv text:** तथाहि–तत्र व्यतिरेकद्वयसहचारेणान्वयव्याप्तिरेव गृह्यते इति। तद्विशिष्टं च पृथिवीत्वं पक्षे गृह्यते। व्याप्तिश्च न साध्यसामानाधिकरण्या-न्तर्भावेन येन फलाभावः।

**Translation:** This can be explained as follows:

In such case, the two negatives form a positive invariable

concomitance. The Earthness qualified by that (positive invariable concomitance) will be known as the property of the subject (i.e. the Earth). In this process the invariable concomitance is not proposed incorporating the co-locatedness with the probandum, in which case, no result (i.e. *sādhya)* would have been left to be known.

**67. lpv text:** सर्वं चैतद्व्यतिरेकिस्थले स्फुटं भविष्यति।

**Translation:** All these things will be cleared in the *Vyatirekavyāpti* chapter.

**68. lpv text:** अन्ये तु तद्विशिष्टपरामर्शस्यानुमितिकारणत्वे विनिगमनामाहुः, इयं धूमव्यक्तिर्वह्निव्याप्या न वेति संशये विपर्यये च तावदनुमितिर्नोत्पद्यत इत्यविवादम्।

**Translation:** Some other logicians say that there is preferential logic with regard to the cause of an inferential cognition which is the confirmatory knowledge of that probans qualified by that (invariable concomitance). There does not arise the inferential cognition from doubt such as 'this particular smoke is pervaded by fire or not' or erroneous knowledge. Here there is no difference of opinion on this point.

**69. lpv text:** तथा च अयं वह्निव्याप्येति ज्ञानेऽनुमितिरुत्पद्यत इति वक्तव्यम्। न च किमर्थं वक्तव्यम्, संशयविपर्ययाभाव एव तत्र कारणमास्तामिति वाच्यम्।

**Translation:** Therefore, one should say that the inferential cognition arises from the knowledge that 'this (particular smoke) is pervaded by fire'. You cannot ask 'why should it be called so?'

**70. lpv text:** तावदभावापेक्षया विशिष्टपरामर्शस्य कारणत्त्वे लाघवात्। विनिगमनाभावेन उभयोः कारणतासम्भवात्।

**Translation:** Because the absence of doubt and erroneous knowledge is the cause there. Therefore, instead of postulating 'n'-number of absences, it is simpler to accept the confirmatory cognition as the cause of an inferential cognition. Since there is no preferential logic both can be postulated as cause.

**71. lpv text:** न च सर्वोपसंहारेण व्याप्तिग्रहानन्तरमियं धूमव्यक्तिर्वह्नि-व्याप्या न वा, न व्याप्येति संशयविपर्ययासम्भवः इति वाच्यम्।

**Translation:** It cannot be also argued that after one gets the knowledge of the invariable concomitance by all conclusive means, it is not possible for him to have either a doubt such as 'the particular smoke is either pervaded by fire or not', or an erroneous knowledge such as 'it is not pervaded' is not possible.

**72. lpv text:** सामान्यनिश्चयस्य सामान्यसंशयविपर्ययप्रतिबन्धक-त्वात्। विशेषसंशयविपर्यययोर्विशेषनिश्चयनिवर्त्तनीयत्वात्।

**Translation:** Because a definite knowledge in general will not set aside a doubt in general and erroneous cognition in general and a doubt in particular or an erroneous knowledge in particular will be removed by a particular definite knowledge.

**73. lpv text:** किञ्च यत्संशयो यत्प्रतिबन्धको भवति तन्निश्चयस्तस्य कारणं भवतीति सामान्यतः सिद्धम्।

**Translation:** Moreover, when the doubt (say, doubt of 'x'), prevents that (the knowledge of that 'x') it is to be accepted that the knowledge of that ('x') is the cause of that. It is generally an established fact.

**74. lpv text:** अत्रापि पक्षधर्मस्य व्याप्यत्वसन्देहादनुमितिर्नोत्पद्यते इत्यवश्यं तत्र पक्षधर्मस्य व्याप्यत्वप्रकारकनिश्चयः कारणं वक्तव्यमिति।

**Translation:** Here also, the inferential cognition does not arise from doubt that 'the property of the subject is pervaded (by fire) or not', and so one must accept that the definite knowledge of the property of the subject, in which 'the pervadedness' appears as qualifier, is the cause.

**75. lpv text:** किं च पर्वतो वह्निव्याप्यवानयमिति शब्दज्ञानानन्तरं वह्न्यनुमितिरुत्पद्यते इत्यविवादम्।

**Translation:** Moreover, there arises the inferential cognition of fire from the Verbal understanding 'The Mountain possesses something (say, smoke) which is pervaded by fire'. There is no difference of opinion regarding this point.

**76. lpv text:** न च तत्र व्याप्यतावच्छेदकः प्रकारो भासत इति अवश्यं पक्षधर्मस्य व्याप्यत्वज्ञानमनुसरणीयम्।

**Translation:** You cannot say that there (in such Verbal understanding), the delimitor of the pervadedness appears as a qualifier. Therefore, one must follow that one has to have the knowledge of the pervadedness of the property of the subject.

**77. lpv text:** न च तत्र व्याप्यस्य व्याप्यत्वमेवावच्छेदकः प्रकारो भासत इति वाच्यम्।

It cannot be said that there i.e. in that Verbal understanding the delimitor of the pervadedness of the pervaded appears as a qualifier.

**78. lpv text:** यद् वह्निव्याप्यवद् भवति तद्वह्निमद् भवतीत्यवश्यमवच्छेदकरूपाया अपरव्याप्तेर्भाने प्रमाणाभावात्।

**Translation:** Because whatever possesses that, which is pervaded by fire, possesses fire. Therefore, there is no definite proof for the knowledge of another invariable concomitance, which can be of the form of the delimitor.

**79. lpv text:** किन्तु तत्रावच्छेद्यरूपैव धूमे वह्निव्याप्तिर्भासत इति।

**Translation:** But in such case, the delimitor of the form of the invariable concomitance of fire alone appears in smoke.

**80. lpv text:** किञ्च तद्भाने वाऽवच्छेदकं व्याप्यत्वमेव भाति तदा सर्वत्र तदेवास्त्विति तृतीयलिङ्गपरामर्शप्रकरणं समाप्तम्।

**Translation:** Moreover, if in that knowledge (in the Confirmatory knowledge arising from that sentence) the delimitor of the pervadedness is accepted as 'the state of being pervaded', then only let the same be accepted in each case of inference. (Thus, it is necessary to postulate the stage of *Parāmarśa* in the process of inferential cognition).

Here ends the chapter called *'Tṛtīyaliṅgaparāmarśa'.*

## FOOTNOTES

1. NSD, edited by B.K. Motilal, p. 21.
2. Ibid.
3. Ibid., p. 11.
4. *Liṅgaparāmarśavādaḥ*.

# BIBLIOGRAPHY

## PRIMARY SOURCES


1. Text : Bṛhati
   System deals with : Mīmāṃsā
   Author : Prabhākara Miśra
   Editor : S.K. Ramanātha Śāstri
   Details : Madras University Sanskrit Series No. 3, University of Madras, 1934
2. Text : Bhāṭṭacintāmaṇi
   System deals with : Mīmāṃsā
   Author : Gāgābhaṭṭa
   Editor : Patawardhan R.
   Details : Babu Haridas Gupta Publication, 1900
3. Text : Mīmāṃsāsūtṛa
   System deals with : Mīmāṃsā
   Author : Jaiminī
   Editor : Dr. Goswami M.
   Details : Tara Book Agency, Baraṇāsi, 1984
4. Text : Mānameyodaya
   System deals with : Mīmāṃsa

| | | | |
|---|---|---|---|
| | Author | : | Nārāyaṇa |
| | Editor | : | C. Kunhan Raja and S.S. Surya-nārāyaṇa |
| | Details | : | Theoshophical publishing house, Madras, 1933 |
| 5. | Text | : | Nyāyabindu |
| | System deals with | : | Buddhism |
| | Author | : | Dharmakirtī |
| | Editor | : | Dr. Srinivasa Śāstri |
| | Details | : | Sahitya Bhandara, Meratha, 1975 |
| 6. | Text | : | Nyāyabodhinī |
| | System deals with | : | Nyāya |
| | Author | : | Govardhanācārya (comm. On Tarkasaṃgraha) |
| | Editor | : | Athalye and Bodas |
| | Details | : | BORI, Poona, 1974 |
| 7. | Text | : | Nayāyamañjarī |
| | System deals with | : | Nyāya |
| | Author | : | Jayanta Bhaṭṭa |
| | Editor | : | K.S. Varadāchārya |
| | Details | : | Oriental Research Institute, Mysore, 1969. |
| 8. | Text | : | Nāyapraveśa |
| | System deals with | : | Buddhism |
| | Author | : | Dignāga |
| | Editor | : | Anandasankara B. Dhruva |
| | Details | : | Oriental Institute, Baroda, 1968. |
| 9. | Text | : | Nyāyaratnākara (Vol. 1) |

| | | | |
|---|---|---|---|
| | System deals with | : | Mīmāṃsā |
| | Author | : | Parthasārathi Miśra |
| | Editor | : | Gajanana Śāstri |
| | Details | : | Bhartiya Vidya Bhavan, 1979 |
| 10. | Text | : | Nyāyasūtra, Bhāṣya, Vārttika, Tatparyaṭīkā, Vṛtti |
| | System deals with | : | Nyāya |
| | Author | : | Gautama, Vātsyāyana, Udyotakara, Vācaspati Miśra, Viśvanātha |
| | Editor | : | Amarendra Chandra Vedālaṃ-kāra |
| | Details | : | Munsiram Monoharalal Pub. Pvt. Ltd., 1985 |
| 11. | Text | : | Nyāyasiddhāntamuktāvalī |
| | System deals with | : | Nyāya |
| | Author | : | Viśvanātha Pañchānana |
| | Editor | : | Ātmārāma Nārāyaṇa Jere |
| | Details | : | Chowkhamba Sanskrit Series Office, Varanasi, 1982 |
| 12. | Text | : | Śāstradīpikā |
| | System deals with | : | Mīmāṃsā |
| | Author | : | Śālikanātha Miśra |
| | Editor | : | Kishordass Swami |
| | Details | : | Sadhubela Sanskrit college, Benaras, 1927. |
| 13. | Text | : | Ślokavārttika |
| | System deals with | : | Mīmāṃsā |
| | Author | : | Kumārila Bhaṭṭa |
| | Editor | : | G.N. Jha |
| | Details | : | Sri Satguru Publication, Delhi, 1983 |

14. Text : Praśastapādabhāṣya
System deals with : Vaiśeṣika
Author : Praśastapādācārya
Editor : Dūrgādhara Jha
Details : Vanaras, 1997

15. Text : Parkaraṇa Pañcikā
System deals with : Mīmāṃsā
Author : Śalikanātha Miśra
Editor : A. Subrahmanyam Śastri
Details : BHU Publication, 1961.

16. Text : Pramāṇavārttika
System deals with : Buddhism
Author : Dharmakirtī
Editor : Swami Dvarikadas Śāstri
Details : Buddha Bharati, Banarasi, 1984

17. Text : Saṃkhyakārikā
System deals with : Sāṃkhya
Author : Iśwarakṛṣṇa
Editor : T. Utpreti
Details : Butala and Co., New Delhi, 1981

18. Text : Sāṃkhyasūtra
System deals with : Sāṃkhya
Author : Kapilamūni
Editor : J.R. Ballantyne
Details : Parimal Publication, Delhi, 1984

| | | | |
|---|---|---|---|
| 19. | Text | : | Sāṃkhyatattvakaumūdī |
| | System deals with | : | Sāṃkhya |
| | Author | : | Vācaspati Miśra |
| | Editor | : | Balaram Udaseen |
| | Details | : | Swami Atama Swarupji Pub. Haridwar, 1931 |
| 20. | Text | : | Syādvādamañjarī |
| | System deals with | : | Jainism |
| | Author | : | Malliṣeṇa Sūri |
| | Details | : | Motilal Banarasi Das, Delhi, 1968 |
| 21. | Text | : | Tarkabhāṣā |
| | System deals with | : | Nyāya |
| | Author | : | Keśava Miśra |
| | Editor | : | Surendradev Śāstri |
| | Details | : | Bharatiya Prakashan, Kanpur, 1976 |
| 22. | Text | : | Tarkāmṛta |
| | System deals with | : | Nyāya |
| | Author | : | Jagadiśa Tarkālaṃkāra |
| | Editor | : | Jiban Kishan Tarkatirtha |
| | Details | : | Asiatic Society, Calcutta, 1974 |
| 23. | Text | : | Tattvacintāmaṇi : (Vol. I and II) |
| | System deals with | : | Nyāya |
| | Author | : | Gaṅgeśa Upādhyāyā |
| | Editor | : | Kāmākhyānātha Tarkavāgiśa |
| | Details | : | Navrang, New Delhi, 1988. |

## SECONDARY SOURCES

*A History of Indian Logic*

—Dr. Satis Chandra Vidyabhushan, M. Banarasidas, Delhi, 1978.

*Anumāna Pramāṇa*

—Dr. Baliram Shukla, Eastern Book linkers, Delhi, 1986.

*Bhāratīya Darśana Bṛhatkoṣa*

—Bachulal Avasthi, Sharada Publishing House, Delhi, 1997.

*Buddhist Logic*

—F. Stcherbatsky, M. M. Publishers Pvt. Ltd., New Delhi, 1984.

*Encyclopedia of Indian Philosophies*

—Karl H. Potter, Matilal Banarasidas, New Delhi, 1977.

*Epistemology of the Bhāṭṭa School of Pūrva Mīmāṁsā*

—Prof. Govardhan P. Bhatta, Chowkhamba Sanskrit Series, Varanasi, 1962.

*History of Indian Epistemology*

—Dr. Jwala Prasad, M. M. Publishers Pvt. Ltd., New Delhi, 1987.

*Indian Logic*

—Dr. B.N. Singh Asha publications, Varanasi, 1988.

*Indian Theory of Knowledge*

—Dr. C.D. Bijalwan, Heritage Publishers, New Delhi, 1977.

*Invariable Concomitance in Navya-Nyāya*

—Prof. Toshihiro Wada, Sri satguru publications, Delhi, 1990.

*Materials for the Study of Navya-Nyāya*

—Prof. H.H. Ingalls, London, 1951.

*The Navya-Nyāya Theory of Knowledge*

—Dr. L.C. Mullati, Karnataka Universiti, Dharwad, 1977.

*The Nyāya Theory of Knowledge*

—Prof. Satischandra Chatarjee, University of Calcutta, 1950.

*Parāmarśa* in *Navya-nyāya* (Ph.D. Thesis)

—Krishna H. Kulakarni, CASS, University of Pune, 1999.

*The Prabhākara School of Pūrva Mīmāṁsā*

—Prof. Ganganatha Jha, Motilal Banarasi Dass, Delhi, 1978.

*Six Ways of Knowing*

—Dr. D.M. Datta, University of Calcutta, 1972.

*Studies in Language, Logic and Epistemology*

—Prof. V.N. Jha, Pratibha Prakashan, New Delhi, 1984.

# INDEX

★★★